WEAPONIZED DRONES TERRORISM IN AFRICA

Al Qaeda, Al Shabaab, Boko Haram and ISIS

WEAPONIZED DRONES TERRORISM IN AFRICA

Al Qaeda, Al Shabaab, Boko Haram and ISIS

By

SARON MESSEMBE OBIA

Vij Books India Pvt Ltd
New Delhi (India)

Published by

Vij Books India Pvt Ltd
(Publishers, Distributors & Importers)
2/19, Ansari Road
Delhi – 110 002
Phones: 91-11-43596460, 91-11-47340674
Mob: 98110 94883
E-mail: contact@vijpublishing.com
Web : www.vijbooks.in

Copyright © 2023, *Author*

ISBN: 978-93-95675-84-0 (Hardback)

ISBN: 978-93-95675-82-6 (Paperback)

ISBN: 978-93-95675-85-7 (ebook)

Price : ₹ 850/-

Dedicated to

Mme Obia Rosaline Efamba B. and Mme Pamela Ayuk Bessong Epse Tchoussoknou

We were scared, but our fear was not as strong as our courage.

-Malala Yousafzai

CONTENTS

FOREWORD

Drones are becoming obliquitous in the annals of humanity. From Military use to civilian use. Why this piece is very important for the policy makers and public to understand. The possibility of drones being used for good superseded its impact on being used for bad and malicious activity. Delivery of medicine and lifesaving means of medical equipment over terrains that regular means of transportation cannot cover. Surveillance of terrains for fighting forest fires to maintaining National Parks from poachers.

That potential for drones is now overshadowed by its potential for harm. Drug dealers from Brazil to Japan now use it to deliver drugs in cities. Assassination attempts on sitting head of state by drones. Terrorists adapting from Africa, Middle East, and Asia. To use of Drones as vehicles of mass destruction.

Governments use drone as the go to mechanization of killing High Value Targets. Warfare now from the Ukraine war to the border wars in Central Asia. Drones are used to change battle conditions. Even tools of terror as witnessed in Kyiv, Ukraine infrastructure attacks by Iranian made drones used by the Russian forces.

The loss of civilian lives raises the questions of morality and legal precedence of the use of this new technology on our human ethics values, military rules, and international laws.

It's a brave new world which this piece brilliantly states the issues clearly. A must read for those who want to know what's next with drones in our world. Under civilian, military, and humanitarian needs of this world.

Mr. Mohamed Ahmed

Founder and Executive Director of Average Mohamed

2020 State Department Citizen of the Year

2018 Citizen Diplomat of the Year Global Ties

Bush Foundation Fellow

PREFACE

The incorporation of drones in security operations, has given a different narrative to counter terrorism and counter-insurgency. States have adopted new security strategies in order to provide solutions to the emerging menace of remote-control warfare; from special operations forces (SOF); unmanned vehicles and autonomous weapons systems; cyber warfare; and intelligence, surveillance and reconnaissance (ISR). Despite successful counter-terrorism operations, civil society has a different narrative on governments' and militaries' actual intentions and capabilities. The cultural divide between civil society and the military in some African countries on technological, political and doctrinal developments concerning lethal autonomous weapons systems and cyber warfare has orchestrated debates, appealing governments to enact reforms on armed drones, mercenaries and mass surveillance.

Al Shabaab and Boko Haram are gaining momentum as the pledge allegiance to transnational organizations like Al Qaeda and ISIS. Despite international and national responses adopted and counterterrorism operations coordinated with drones, these groups fatwa and aspiration for a self-proclaim Caliphate still remain their major agenda. As long as nations continually eliminate leaders and maintain an intelligence advantage, the menace of terrorism is compatible. Inspiration, leadership, fatwa and tactics cannot defeat education, technology and democracy.

ACKNOWLEDGMENTS

I want to thank Mr. Jean Marie Tchoussoknou and Mr. Charles Ebune for their financial support and coaching. Intelligentsia and wisdom are words used to describe fellows, as Dr. Prof. Ivan Tkach, Brig. Gen. Pradip K. Vij, Col. (R) Youssa Gedeon, Major (R) Tchassom, Mr. Noor Dahri and Mr. Alvin Odinukwe, whose good conversations inspired me to ask more questions, and challenge more ideas.

I am grateful to Mme Ethel Edimo Endale, Mr. Obia Ranndy, Mr. Modika M. Daniel, Mr. Obia Mboni Bryan, Mr. Obia Remmy B., Mr. Mbunwo Tanue E., Mr. Bright N. Shey Tamfuh, Miss Mirabel Konglim, Miss Eyambe Diale Bergitta, and Miss Tina Brenda Koti A., for their critics and resilience behaviour which prompted my ink to the final word of this book.

List of Acronyms and Abbreviations

AAR	After action report
ADIZ	Air Defense Identification Zone
AGL	Above Ground Level
ATC	Air Traffic Control
AFRICOM	U.S. Africa Command
AQAP	Al-Qaeda in the Arabian Peninsula
AQIM	Al-Qaeda in the Islamic Maghreb
ASM	Air-to-Surface Missile
AUMF	Authorization for the Use of Military Force
BDA	Battle Damage Assessment
BIJ	Bureau of Investigative Journalism
BPC	Building Partner Capacity
CALL	Center for Army Lessons Learned
CENTCOM	U.S. Central Command
BVLOS	Beyond Visual Line-Of-Sight
CBP	Customs and Border Protection
COTS	Commercial-Off-The-Shelf
C-UAS	Counter Unmanned Aerial System
CIA	Central Intelligence Agency
CIVCAS	Civilian Casualties
CIV K	Civilians Killed

CNA	Center for Naval Analyses
COIN	Counterinsurgency
COMISAF	Commander, International Security Assistance Force
CPA	Coalition Provisional Authority
CT	Counterterrorism
DEA	Drug Enforcement Agency
DHS	Department of Homeland Security
DJI	Dajiang Innovation
DoD	Department of Defense
DNI	Director of National Intelligence
DOJ	Department of Justice
DPH	Directly Participate In Hostilities
EOF	Escalation of Force
EUFOR	European Union Force
FAA	Federal Aviation Administration
FARC	Fuerzas Armadas Revolucionarias de Colombia or the Revolutionary Armed Forces of Colombia—People's Army
FATA	Federally Administered Tribal Areas
FBI	Federal Bureau of Investigation
FISA	Foreign Intelligence Surveillance Act
FMS	Foreign Military Sales
FOIA	Freedom of Information Act
HSE	Homeland Security Enterprise
HUMINT	Human intelligence
ICAO	International Civil Aviation Organization

ICE	Immigration and Customs Enforcement
IED	Improvised Explosive Device
IAC	International Armed Conflict
ICRC	International Committee of the Red Cross
IED	Improvised Explosive Device
IHL	International Humanitarian Law
IHRL	International Human Rights Law
ISAF	International Security Assistance Force
ISIL	Islamic State of Iraq and the Levant (a.k.a. IS, ISIS)
ISIS	Islamic State
ISR	Intelligence, Surveillance, Reconnaissance
JCCS	Joint Civilian Casualty Study
JCOA	Joint and Coalition Operational Analysis Division/Joint Center for Operational Analysis
JLLIS	Joint Lessons Learned Information System
JIDO	Joint Improvised Threat-defeat Organization
KIA	Killed in Action
LOAC	Law of Armed Conflict
NAS	National Airspace System
NAF	New America Foundation
NATO	North Atlantic Treaty Organization
NCT	Nation Containing the Target
NGO	Nongovernmental organization
NIAC	Non international Armed Conflict
NSA	National Security Agency

OEF	Operation Enduring Freedom
OME	Operational military effectiveness
OPE	Operational preparation of the environment
OSD	Office of the Secretary of Defense
PED	Processing, exploitation, and dissemination
PID	Positive Identification
POW	Prisoner of War
PPG	Presidential Policy Guidance
POE	Point-Of-Entry
PTDS	Persistent Threat Detection System
QRF	Quick Reaction Force
ROE	Rules of engagement
RAID	Rapid Aerostat Initial Deployment
SAMS	Surface-To-Air Missile System
SBI	Secure Borders Initiative
SA	Situational Awareness
SERE	Survival, Evasion, Resistance, and Escape training
SME	Strategic military effectiveness
SOF	Special Operations Forces
TARS	Tethered Aerostat Radar System
TCO	Transnational Criminal Organization
TLAM	Tomahawk land attack missile
TMA	Traditional military activity
TME	Tactical military effectiveness
TTP	Tactics, techniques, and procedures

TSA	Transportation Security Administration
UA	Unmanned Aircraft
UAV	Unmanned Aerial Vehicle
UAS	Unmanned Aerial System
UCMJ	Uniformed Code of Military Justice
UN	United Nations
UNMISS	United Nations Mission in South Sudan
UNOCI	United Nations Operation in Côte d'Ivoire
UNSCR	United Nations Security Council Resolution
USAID	U.S. Agency for International Development
VLOS	Visual Line-Of-Sight
WMD	Weapons of Mass Destruction

Chapter One

Introduction

The proliferation of technological devices in counter-terrorism operations in the Sahel region have increased radicalization, and undermined democratic principles and human rights. The high number of civilian casualties in drone strikes has re-oriented the security discourse on the supposed accuracy of this 'precision warfare tool'.

Despite a high budget oriented towards drones, these remote control tools are tactics for countering terrorism and counter-insurgency operations. Drone Market projections suggest that the global annual export market for UAVs is likely to grow from \$942 million to \$2.3 billion over the decade from 2013 to 2023[1]. More so, estimation for 2017 worldwide UAV production revealed it could average about 960 unmanned aircraft annually[2].

Experts suggest that it is necessary for the United States of America to cooperate with Russia in order to fight terrorism. This aligns with President Putin's suggestion to the United

---

[1] https://www.militaryaerospace.com/unmanned/article/16719224/global-uav-market-to-reach-23-billion-by-2023-chinese-company-to-be-largest-uav-builder

[2] Idries et al (2015) Challenges of Developing UAV Applications: A Project Management View. Proceedings of the 2015 International Conference on Industrial Engineering and Operations Management Dubai, United Arab Emirates (UAE), March 3 – 5, 2015.

States to set aside their differences over Syria, Ukraine, Venezuela, and other matters, get down to the business, and engage in the global war on terrorism.

Other scholars consider Russian to be a menace to the U.S, and their counter-terrorism strategy is contrary to each country's values and national security interests. Some Western experts equally argue that, Russia's geopolitical objectives are to weaken the United States, fragment the transatlantic community, and delegitimize international norms of human rights and democracy. To accomplish these aims, Russia supports neo-Nazi hate groups to sow discord in European societies. She's equally accused of spreading fake conspiracy theories to radicalize Americans against their immigrant neighbours and coworkers. With regard to international relations, a change in the 'rule of the game' between Russia and the United States would be peace and security for the world.

The use of Drone by Violent Non-State Actors (VNSAs)

With the fragmentation of states, the quest by some groups to proclaim self-caliphate and the development of new weapons for counter-terrorism and insurgency, these weapons are equally used by VNSAs. It is necessary to understand the historical background of drone use by VNSAs. Japanese terror group *Aum Shinrikyo*, was among the first to perpetrate and attack using drones to distribute sarin gas against civilian populations[3]. In the Middle East, terrorist groups use consumer drones to carry out reconnaissance missions. With the global menace posed by terrorist groups in the 21st century, and based on the fact that drone technology is

---

3   Read; Miniature Menace: The Threat of Weaponized Drone Use by Violent Non-state Actors by Thomas Braun https://www.airuniversity.af.edu/Wild-Blue-Yonder/Article-Display/Article/2344151/miniature-menace-the-threat-of-weaponized-drone-use-by-violent-non-state-actors/

cheap and easy to operate, many different VNSAs are able to acquire and use drones for reconnaissance operations and coordinated attacks.

In 2013, the ***Shiite Muslim terror group Hezbollah*** reportedly dropped two small explosive devices on Syrian rebel strongholds using a drone supplied by Iran (Fleiss and Braun, 2020). Most groups in the 21st century are state-sponsored, which facilitate the acquisition of military unmanned aerial systems (UAS), by simply modifying commercial drones. The modification to war drones for combat usually requires knowledge and resources.

In 2015, Kurdish fighters in Syria shot down several commercial drone laden with explosives, which belong to ISIL[4]. A year later, ISIL newsletter "al-Naba" revealed that a unit for "Unmanned Aircraft of the Mujahideen" was to engineer UASs for the group to deploy in combat. ISIL continued with the development of its drone technology, increasing the capabilities of its drones and finding innovative ways to use drones.

In 2017, ISIL adopted deception and creativity patterns to increase the number of casualties with drone attacks[5]. The Kurdish force's response to terrorist activities in not slow, as they continue to shoot down surveillance drones of VNSA and take them back to a coalition base for examination. While being disassembled, the booby-trapped drone exploded, killing two Kurdish fighters and wounding two French soldiers. According to Fleiss and Braun (2020), several operations were carried out by coalition forces to regain Mosul in June 2017, in which ISIL flew several powered

---

4   Ibid

5   https://www.airuniversity.af.edu/Wild-Blue-Yonder/Article-Display/ Article/2344151/miniature-menace-the-threat-of-weaponized-drone-use- by-violent-non-state-actors/

drone against the latter every month. UAS technology are weaponized by ISIL and other Islamic terror groups in the Middle East and even far beyond the region.

Apart from terrorist organizations, cartel groups across Central and South America have been caught with drones in their possession. They mainly use drones to smuggle narcotics and other illegal goods and have not carried out any violent attacks with them, military and intelligence agencies have found drones believed to be used in weaponized attacks. However, they are not the only groups to have access to drone technology.

Political opposition groups have been accused of plotting and attempting to use drones to assassinate government leaders across the U.S. During a presidential articulation by Venezuelan Nicolás Maduro on 4 August 2018, at a military parade in front of thousands of civilians and military personnel, the ceremony was interrupted by the sound of two loud explosions above the crowd[6]. Assailants used two DJI M-600 commercial drones laden with a small camera and C4 explosives in an attempt to assassinate the president[7]. However, neither drone attack reached its target successfully. One of the drones crashed into an apartment complex and exploded on the ground two blocks away. The second drone came closer. It exploded less than a football field away from Maduro, above the crowd but within his line of sight[8]. The failed attack on Maduro and injuries inflicted to seven

---

6   https://www.nytimes.com/video/world/americas/100000006042079/how-the-drone-attack-on-maduro-unfolded-in-venezuela.html

7   DJI – Based out of Shenzhen, China, DJI it is the world's leading producer of consumer drone technology.

8   Christoph Koettl and Barbara Marcolini, "A Closer Look at the Drone Attack on Maduro in Venezuela," New York Times, 10 August 2018, www.nytimes.com/2018/08/10/world/americas/venezuela-video-analysis.html.

soldiers, exposed the threat that drones pose in the hands of capable VNSAs.

Nowourdays is common for thousands of flights to be delayed or canceled as major airports across the globe are forced to ground aircraft because a drone is posing a threat to flight safety. Al-Qaida has even taken inspiration from these events. Intelligence agencies have intercepted the group's plans to use drones to take down airliners using explosive-laden drones at airports in the U.S. and the UK. A state of emergency was declared in the city of Paris after unidentified drones were spotted being flown across the capital city shortly after the devastating **Charlie Hebdo terror attacks**[9]. In the U.S., the White House was placed on lockdown after a drone was illegally flying within city limits and it crashed onto the White House lawn[10].

The Justification for Violent Non-State Actors Use Drones

Weaponized drone technology is a game-changer for an organization and contemporary warfare. Typically, the older, experienced VNSAs have the capability of operating a drone program. To better combat the rising threat of weaponized drone use by terror groups, one must understand the motivations behind when and why these actors use them to their advantage. VNSAs use drones for surveillance just like the military. In the past few years, they resort to purchasing and modifying off-the-shelf consumer parts drone to coordinated attacks.

Documents recovered from ISIL buffer zone revealed how they were able to acquire drones. It equally exposed, most of the drones used by the latter were not very sophisticated,

---

9   ibid

10 Drone That Crashed at White House Was Quadcopter. https://time.com/3682307/white-house-drone-crash/

but simple DIY techniques, combine high- and low-tech components purchased from various connections across Asia and Europe[11]. To acquire these parts of these drones, the group used the centralized and bureaucratic framework that it already had in place from its acquisition of other weapons. In order to work on the program two brothers from Asia were solicited and who recruited other operatives to work alongside them. Their scheme led to the creation of several shell companies to acquire consumer drones from manufacturers in Asia, the US, and Canada and, when possible, using sites such as PayPal and fake aliases[12].

This scheme facilitated the use other shell companies to purchase stand-alone components such as cameras and GPS units before activating them in the US or Europe. They used another set of shell companies to ship the drones to ISIL affiliates worldwide. The intricate web of companies and bank accounts made the drones hard to trace and appear as if the purchasers were just hobbyists.

Report from the Combating Terrorism Center at West Point revealed that "these purchases, which were essentially delivered to a town right next to the Islamic State's doorstep, illustrate just how easy it was for Islamic State operatives to obtain drone components from Western retailers at the time."[13] The capture and killing of some members by drone strike, did not relent the groups effort in the acquisition of drones in order to fight back.

---

11 Elena Pérez (2014) Meaningful connections: exploring the usesof telematic technology in performance. Liminalities: A Journal of Performance StudiesVol. 10, No. 1, May 2014

12 ibid

13 Don Rassler, The Islamic State and Drones: Supply, Scale, and Future Threats (West Point, New York: Combating Terrorism Center, 2018), https://ctc. usma.edu/wp-content/uploads/2018/07/Islamic-State-and-Drones-Release-Version.pdf.

ISIL demonstrated that a VNSA could overcome the hurdles and export restrictions that allowed it to acquire hobby drones and transform them into deadly tools of war. While the technology helped tilt the asymmetric balance of powers it faced, it is not the only factor that plays into when and why groups will develop and use weaponized drones. Whenever a state or group uses new technology in warfare, it often receives a harsher response from its opponents because it is viewed as an escalation of warfare. Therefore, the group must be capable and willing to dedicate more manpower and willpower to up the fighting.

U.S. global war on terror has been join by other states, forming a military coalition to fight Islamic terrorism after attacks on respective countries. The menace posed by terror groups is gradually reducing as repercussions from the coalition increases. For example, the coalition response to ISIL's use of weaponized drones included the targeted bombing of all locations believed to be used by ISIL for drone development.

Drones not only elicit a more severe response but also pose a threat to a group's standing and capabilities. This is based on the fact that, drones used over the years made ISIL powerful. When coalition forces ramped up the fight against ISIL, it led to its downfall. Once it fell and was severely weakened, it stopped using drones not because it was more challenging to acquire, but because it could not face the consequences that came alongside their use.

One of the most important factors for terror organizations is their image because they use it for recruitment. The group's recruiters depend on the group projecting a powerful image through social media and the internet to contact potential new members usually troubled young males across the world. Therefore, when its image weakens, it loses the ability to seduce people onto their side. To strengthen their image, terror groups often perform violent attacks, like suicide bombings, against civilian populations to ignite fear into minds and gain more publicity and recognition. The more deadly and vicious the attack showcased by a sophisticated social media capability the greater publicity, name recognition, and credibility the group achieves. This, in turn, builds a strong reputation. When used properly, weaponized consumer drones can be a deadly instrument in the hands of VNSAs. A failed attack, especially with new technology like drones, will weaken the group's image. Drones, as any other new technology, bring a set of unique growing pains as the group learns how to use the technology both tactically and strategically. Therefore, the use of weaponized drones by VNSAs requires operational expertise to coordinate an attack and recover from the consequences that come with it.

Counterterrorism strategy to combat the new wave of insecurity

With the changing dynamics of armed conflicts and internal wrangling around the world, it is important to provide a general distinction between counterterrorism and counterinsurgency[14]. Counterterrorism and counterinsurgency are two different styles of warfare; counterterrorism focuses on the enemy while counterinsurgency focuses on the population. Most at times, counterterrorism involves disrupting terrorists' ability to conduct operations while counterinsurgency often involves building and solidifying domestic institutions and society against negative torts. However, these two forms of warfare are usually counteracting, produce a variety of potential threats. U.S. drone program is criticized by some Pakistani civilians based in Waziristan, because of the mass civilian casualties after strikes. As a result, roughly three fourths of Pakistanis conclude that the U.S. is Pakistan's primary antagonist.

---

14 Read ;Drone Warfare as a Military Instrument of Counterterrorism Strategy by Second Lieutenant ALexander Farrow, uSaF. https://www.airuniversity. af.edu/Portals/10/ASPJ_Spanish/Journals/Volume-28_Issue-4/2016_4_02_ farrow_s_eng.pdf

Evidently, the topic of drone warfare is vast, and in order to limit the scope to analyze drone warfare solely in the light of counterterrorism strategy, not counterinsurgency strategy, the work shall refrain from elaborating on many of the important offsetting effects, such as civilian casualties, foreign sentiment. These require more comprehensive review on national strategy, as a multitude of other military technology may also produce these offsetting effects. Analysis will focus on the use of drones to combat terrorist organizations and how these organizations weaponized drones. Counterterrorism involves two phases of disrupting terrorist operations:

(1) identifying the threat and

(2) eliminating the threat[15].

Firstly, a nation must seek out the enemy combatants through intelligence. Secondly, a nation must take aggressive action against the combatants, forcing the terrorists to disperse deeper into the shadows to avoid being a target. Thus, the target nation must once again seek out the combatants through intelligence so that it can take aggressive action in the future. In that sense, counterterrorism is cyclical, with intelligence leading to strikes.

Identifying the Threat: Intelligence, Surveillance, and Reconnaissance

The Intelligence Cycle

The mutation of terrorist activities made the CIA to conclude that, terrorism often does not originate from a single aggressor or location. Rather, the threat is often multilateral and international. It is challenging to comply eradicate a

---

15 Drone Warfare as a Military Instrument of Counterterrorism Strategy by Second Lieutenant Alexander Farrow, USAF. https://www.airuniversity. af.edu/Portals/10/ASPJ_Spanish/Journals/Volume-28_Issue-4/2016_4_02_ farrow_s_eng.pdf

terrorist organization because a nation cannot be able to assess from where or whom the next threat will emerge. From the **USS Cole attack** to the **Fort Hood shootings** to the **Boston Marathon bombing**[16], individuals everywhere in the world, including US citizens, can wage terror against a civilian population. Furthermore, sovereignty of states are continuously challenged by violent non-state actors with the prevalence of technological weapons. For example, al Qaeda adaptation to new technologies and management systems is challenging to by United States intelligence services.

Intelligence is one of the most effective strategy to combat terrorism. The global war on terror requires knowledge or data that has been gathered to respond to particular questions, verify situations, and provide understanding to particular events. Targeted intelligence is gathered from any number of sources and refined through synthesis and analysis before dissemination to the appropriate channel for subsequent action. This process is known as the intelligence cycle and is essential for identifying the terrorist network.

Aerial Reconnaissance

One of the most effective tool for intelligence, surveillance and counter espionage is a drone. According to USAF testimonials, about 97% of mission time is dedicated purely to reconnaissance[17]. Nonetheless, aircraft also contributes to the intelligence cycle as its always collects and distributes information. Specifically, it collects intelligence efficiently via advanced visual equipment and long loiter capabilities. Predator and the Reaper drones are equipped with high definition and thermal cameras on the undersides of their

---

16 ibid

17 "Drones: What Are They and How Do They Work?" BBC News. N.p., n.d. Web. 02 Dec. 2014. <http://www.bbc.com/news/world-south-asia-10713898>.

fuselages. These cameras are powerful enough to zoom and read the license number on a driver's ID card. Pilots use the cameras' high-power-red capabilities when searching for and following potential targets. These aircraft are usually used to collects useful intelligence about the behavioural patterns of the enemy while flying at a high altitude, and unseen to the target.

Furthermore, aerial imagery technology is vastly improving. For example, the US Air Force is experimenting with a high-tech camera system known as the Gorgon Stare. The Gorgon Stare essentially combines the visual capacity of multiple advanced cameras, allowing the aircraft to observe areas that are 4 kilometers in diameter. US Air Force Reaper drones are already been equipped with this new system, allowing pilots and intelligence analysts to observe parts of entire cities at one time. In this way, the drone is highly effective for gathering a large amount of visual data.

Most drones loiters in the air longer than a conventional manned aircraft, maximizing reconnaissance time, since it has no pilot or a cockpit, the weight of the aircraft is significantly minimized. The Predator drone, can fly an average of 24 hours, which helps in combat air patrols in order to ensure constant surveillance. Each combat air patrol consists of four alternating aircraft. Typically, one aircraft acquires intelligence, one flies back to base for refueling, one refuels at the base, and one flies to relieve the operational drone. In this way, drone operators can ensure that the aircraft loiters as long as possible over a given area, increasing the chance that intelligence analysts will identify a target. The images collected from 'eyes in the sky' aircraft are transmitted via satellite to pilots at Air Force bases in the United States, like **Creech AFB**. Based on the fact that, the entire process is electronic, intelligence feeds can be stopped, played, rewound, and fast-forwarded from virtually anywhere in the world that has a connection to the satellite link. In the U.S., the Joint Special Operations Command (JSOC) or the CIA have the power to view the drone feed and provide guidance through networked chatting channels.

A drone, therefore does not only surveys the battlefield, but it also distributes intelligence in order to counter terrorism. Two specific counterterrorism operations highlight the intelligence-gathering capabilities of drones. These case studies were chosen because they are high-profile examples of identifying the location of prominent leaders of terrorist organizations like al Qaeda in Iraq and Boko Haram in West Africa.

Case one: Abu Mosab al-Zarqawi

Second Lieutenant Alexander Farrow, USAF described Abu Musab al-Zarqawi, a "raw psychopathic killer born for a war without moral limits on brutality", terrorized Fallujah, Iraq[18]. Following jihadist tendencies; beheading and abductions of persons, which made US Air Force deployed dozens of Predator aircraft to scan the streets and alleyways of the city in search of Zarqawi. A Predator drone was used to identify the building in which Zarqawi was hiding, relaying that information to nearby F-16C aircraft, which obliterated the target.

Case two: Osama bin Laden

The most publicized counter-terrorism operation, is the raid on Osama bin Laden's compound in Abbottabad, Pakistan in 2011. Before the raid, the CIA had allegedly flew bat-like RQ-170 stealth drone over the suspected compound, using thermal imaging to identify the possibility that Osama bin Laden resided in the building. The imagery helped intelligence

---

18 https://www.airuniversity.af.edu/Portals/10/ASPJ_Spanish/Journals/
    Volume-28_Issue-4/2016_4_02_farrow_s_eng.pdf

analysts confirm a possible profile of the terrorist leader. During the raid on Osama bin Laden's compound, President Obama and his national security team were able to directly watch the events unfold via a live RQ-170 drone feed. The RQ-170 helped to locate the target and updated command and control on the progression of the special operations raid. The aircraft was unmanned, it minimized responsibility and lives in the case that the aircraft was discovered during the operation. The aircraft efficiently helped expose Osama bin Laden's portrait.

Eliminating the Threat: Aerial Strikes

Offensive Counterterrorism

The global war on terror requires eliminating the threat from the battlefield. According to Boyle, terrorism is a dynamic, asymmetric form of warfare that requires aggressive, precise action against the organization. In President Obama's words, "battlefields have evolved and changed", and therefore, it is necessary to take preemptive action in order to eliminate the possibility of a terrorist attack. "We must disrupt al Qaeda's terrorist planning before it gets anywhere near our homeland or our citizens". Aggressive, preemptive action, therefore, must be taken in order to eliminate the threat and the impact of UAV include everything from freezing financial assets, detention, and lethal strikes. Drones have been particularly effective at lethally eliminating top terrorist leadership.

Eliminating leadership is highly effective at disorganizing the terrorist organization. 'Decapitation' of the terrorist organization depends on two factors:

(1) the terrorist leaders' importance and

(2) difficult succession.

One of the key instrument in to radicalization and emergence of terrorist organizations is doctrine and fatwa of their leaders. Terrorist organizations do not abide to any established moral or social norms, the leaders have significant influence over the creation of norms within the organization. According to Price, removing these leaders from a position of authority is the most significant variable in the downfall of a terrorist organization. This argument has however been challenged, following the death of profile leaders like Osama Ben Laden and Abubakar Shekau.

More so, leadership succession is usually challenging within terrorist organizations. Most organizations are violent, clandestine, and value-based, as such authority is less likely to be institutionalized and legitimate. Rather, leadership is dependent on the charisma of the leader; "charisma is the warrior's basis of authority". No two leaders are the same, so eliminating one leader significantly changes the strategy of the organization as a whole.

The death of Osama bin Laden of al Qaeda is described by Jenkins as a "serious blow" to its capacity because of his inspirational, organizational, and financial advice. Even though bin Laden was more of a figurehead than an active terrorist operative, he symbolized the unification of al Qaeda and set strategic direction for the organization as a whole. His death delegitimized the organization.

Aerial Elimination of Terrorist Leadership

Counterterrorism drones are equipped to eliminate targets based on the programming and sensitivity. The Predator are equipped with AIM-92 Stinger air-to-air and AGM-114 Hellfire air-to-ground missiles. Meanwhile the AGM-114 Hellfire missile is a precise, laser guided armament designed to eliminate an individual militant or a group of militants. Drone pilots learn not only how to deploy these weapons but also learn how to utilize each weapon effectively. The angle of attack, airspeed, and nature of the threat are all factors that lead to the decision of how to deploy the drone's capabilities effectively.

The camera on the Predator drone has a complementary laser system that can be deployed remotely by a sensor operator. This camera can "paint" the target with the laser and the pilot can either chose to fire laser-guided Hellfire missiles or cooperate with another aircraft that will launch a similar attack. The F-16C aircraft that bombed Zarqawi's compound 'cooperated' its laser-guided bomb with the laser that had been engaged from the loitering Predator drone. The drone employs and enables strikes. There are several examples of how drones are effective at eliminating terrorists.

Case One: Anwar al Awlaki

Anwar al Awlaki an American-born jihadist who led an aggressive rhetorical jihad campaign was a casualty of a drone counterterrorism operation. Awlaki grew up in New Mexico, studied civil engineering at Colorado State University[19], and began preaching jihadi violence shortly after 9/11[20]. Awake moved to Yemen to revamp his online rhetorical campaign. Because of his extensive familiarity with American culture, Awlaki's usefulness centred around his ability to attract and appeal to domestic terrorists within the US. His sermons inspired terrorists like those responsible for the *Fort Hood Shooting (2009)*, *the Christmas Day Bombing (2009)*, and the *Times Square Bombing (2010)*. In September 2011, two Predator drones spotted Awlaki in his vehicle, and the CIA

---

19 Shane, Scott; Souad Mekhennet (May 8, 2010). "Anwar al-Awlaki – From Condemning Terror to Preaching Jihad". The New York Times. Archived from the original on May 11, 2010. Retrieved May 9, 2010.

20 https://www.nytimes.com/2015/08/30/magazine/the-lessons-of-anwar-al-awlaki.html

ordered the aircraft to fire Hellfire missiles at it, killing the American jihadist[21].

In President Obama's words, the "death of Awlaki is a major blow to al Qaeda's most active operational affiliate... [he] took the lead in planning and directing efforts to murder innocent Americans."[22] By killing Awlaki, the US eliminated a serious threat that could have continued to inspire others with growing online rhetoric. No al Qaeda leader has since held as much moral influence over homegrown terrorists as Awlaki. As a result, it seems that al Qaeda struggles to replace decimated leaders. Although leaders like Awlaki are hard to replace influentially, it can be even more difficult for the organization to physically replace dead leaders quickly enough to ensure operations run smoothly.

Case two: Baitullah Mehsud

Baitullah Mehsud was member of the Waziristan and considered to be Pakistan's most feared[23]. Orchestrating guerilla terrorist plots since 2005, he subsequently gained international attention with the **Red Mosque siege in Islamabad** (2007)[24]. In August 2009, however, it was reported that Mehsud had succumbed to fatal injuries caused by a CIA Predator strike[25] targeting the leadership of his Taliban cell, which the latter's death was considered impactful, as it fractured chain of command.

Following his death, there were claims that a violent struggle for power took place between the legitimate successor,

---

21   Ibid

22   https://military-history.fandom.com/wiki/Anwar_al-Awlaki

23   https://www.reuters.com/article/us-pakistan-violence-idU-SISL12917120080624

24   https://www.nytimes.com/2007/07/10/world/asia/10pakistan.html

25   https://www.airuniversity.af.edu/Portals/10/ASPJ_Spanish/Journals/Volume-28_Issue-4/2016_4_02_farrow_s_eng.pdf

Hakimullah Mehsud, and Wali-ur-Rehman. Hakimullah Mehsud emerged as the successor, with Rehman as his deputy in command. Both individuals were killed in coordinated attacks by Predator drones in 2013, crippling al Qaeda's chain of command and organizational stability once again.

Osama bin Laden's close advisor, several years earlier, commented on the drone war obliterating al Qaeda's chain of command when he warned that because of aggressive action against leaders in Waziristan, "fighters were being killed faster than they could be replaced". Aggressively and constantly disrupting leadership results in uncoordinated terrorist strategy. By targeting leaders, therefore, drones not only eliminate rhetorical fuel for terrorist fire, but also disrupt strategic focus and operations.

United States of America Drone utilization narrative

One of the major events that have orchestrated a paradigm shift in military operations, particularly that on counter terrorism is the 9/11 attacks on the united states of America. This appeals to the 2001 law authorizing the use of military force against those responsible for the September 11 attacks allow the United States to use drones against a terrorist organization that did not exist on September 11, 2001 (Al-Shabaab & Boko Haram) in a country with no connection to the September 11 attacks and with which the United States is not at war (Somalia, Cameroon)? This is a strategic question which need to be reviewed by the African union peace and security panel.

One of the major scholar's to analyze U.S. strategy, particularly the incorporation of drones in theatre warfare is Professor Koh. The latter use three stance to explain the lawfulness of a drone strike by the U.S. government:

whether the government's action is consistent with domestic law and international law an issue which, in turn, is based on both the law of going to war (jus ad bellum) and the law of conducting a war (*jus in bello*); whether the rights of the targeted person have been adequately considered under domestic and international law; and whether the sovereignty of the country where the killing occurred was adequately considered[26].

Professor Koh[27] reveals that, international law consists of various treaties, including Article 24 of the United Nations ("U.N.") Charter, which contains the general proscription against incursions on sovereignty, Article 51 of the U.N. Charter, which addresses self-defence, and international humanitarian treaties such as the Geneva Conventions of 1949. There also are three bodies of relevant domestic law: (a) the Constitution; (b) statutory law, such as the 2001 Authorization for the Use of Military Force (often referred to as the "AUMF");1 and (c) executive branch policy guidance. Although the executive's policy guidance is classified, various officials have outlined the broad terms in a series of public speeches.

Another legal problematic is that of use of drones outside established theaters of armed conflict. It is necessary to understand that, the United States is in an armed conflict, under the AUMF, with the Taliban, Al-Qaeda and their associated forces. Drone strikes in Afghanistan and adjacent regions can fall within the law of armed conflict, but the United States has gone further and also asserted, under self-defence principles, the right to use force against senior

---

26 Drone Strikes and TargetedKillings: Domestic and International Perspectives. https://www.ca2.uscourts.gov/docs/jc_reports/2014/4_Drone_Strikes.pdf

27 Drone Strikes and Targeted Killings: Domestic and International Perspectives

members of terrorist groups with whom there is no armed conflict.

U.S. modus operandi and the current drone warfare

The secret of US drone wars

The Intercept, a whistleblowing website comparable to Wikileaks, published four important US military documents in October 2014, which revealed the use of drones constituting the US answer to terrorist acts[28]. The documents which were classified and considered secret, illustrated the explosive potential of the information they contain[29]. One document provided details of *Operation HAYMAKER* in Afghanistan. In which two Afghan provinces witnessed a total of sixty individual operations against Taliban fighters. In 56 cases, a Kinetic Strike were carried out with illicit weapons[30].

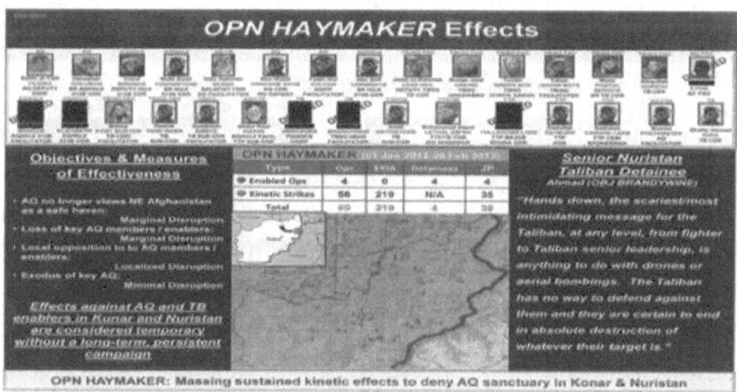

Source: The Intercept (2015)[31]

---

28 The Intercept, 'The Drone Papers', https://theintercept.com/drone-papers/.

29 Current drone warfare in the light of the prohibition of interventions: The use of drones in armed conflicts in Afghanistan, Iraq, Israel, Yemen, Libya, Mali, Pakistan, the Philippines, Somalia, and Syria by Markus Reisner https://viennalawreview.com/index.php/vlr/article/view/52/25

30 Ibid

31 https://theintercept.com/document/2015/10/15/operation-haymaker/

These strikes conducted with the use of armed MQ-1 Predator und MQ-9 Reaper UCAVs. In these attacks, a total of 219 persons were classified as ***Enemy Killed in Action***. Four other operations led to the capture of four more persons[32]. In an interrogation, one of them, a mid-level Taliban commander captured by US special forces during ***Operation BRANDYWINE***, stated the following on the use of US drone strikes against his fighters (translation):

[…] the scariest/most intimidating message for the Taliban, at any level, from fighter to senior leadership, is anything to do with drones or aerial bombing. The Taliban has no way to defend against them and they are certain to end in the absolute destruction of whatever their target is[33].

Classified secret documents published revealed the political leadership of the USA stance that, targeted killings is a highly effective tool for counter terrorism. The Intercept equally revealed other strategic sources which deal with US operations in the Horn of Africa.

Furthermore, the US documents revealed that, the operations were highly successful and need to be expanded to other countries which solicited her help in responding to such menace. It was revealed that all what is required for striking a High Value Target or a High Value Individual is a Positive Identification to the extent of near certainty. As such identification of the target individual does not require 100% certainty. SEC. 2. Authorization for Use Of United States Armed Forces (a) provides ultimate responsibility for this rests with the President of the United States[34].

---

32 https://viennalawreview.com/index.php/vlr/article/view/52/25

33 David Rohde, 'My Guards Absolutely Feared Drones: Reflections on Being Held Captive for Seven Months by the Taliban', in 'Drone Wars, Transforming Conflict, Law and Policy' Peter L. Bergen and Daniel Rothenberg (eds.), (New York: 2015), pp. 9-11.

34 https://www.congress.gov/107/plaws/publ40/PLAW-107publ40.pdf

During the Bush Administration, from 2001 to 2008, a total of 48 targeted killings by means of drones, meanwhile the Obama Administration, between 2009 and 2013 alone, 307 such attacks were documented and about 122 were carried out in 2010, representing a massive increase[35]. AUMF is the American legal basis for the fight against terrorism and the use of drones, as authorized by both Houses of Congress a week after September 11, 2001.

AUMF authorizes the President [...] to use necessary and appropriate force against those nations, organizations, or persons he determines planned, authorized, committed, or aided the terrorist attacks that occurred on 11 September 2001, or harboured such organizations or persons.

This empowered President Obama to apply liberally targeted killing via drones which were used exclusively by the military for the specific operation (Afghanistan and Iraq), and the CIA increasingly became interested. This resulted in military operators using the drones they piloted to carry out missions for the CIA, civilian intelligence service[36].

US have operational drone bases in the Middle East and in Africa. She equally coordinates operations with drones in Pakistan, Yemen, and Somalia. Terror organizations such as the Somali Al-Shabaab Militia now also found themselves in the crosshairs. Whether or not a target individual had actually been identified became less important, and there was a deliberate decision to tolerate potential civilian casualties, i.e. collateral damage.

Consequently, civilian casualties are highly questionable from a moral point of view, in theatre operations. The adoption of the term **signature strike** is to legitimize drone operational

---

35 https://viennalawreview.com/index.php/vlr/article/view/52/25

36 Jeremy Scahill, Dirty Wars: The World is a Battlefield, (New York: Notion Books, 2013), pp. 45-8.

attacks[37]. In 2012, President Obama authorized the CIA and the JSOC, the two entities mandated in the *Global War on Terror*, to fight targets on the basis of their signatures. This referred to a target individual's behaviour pattern, which was collated on the basis of wiretapped telephone conversations, accessible human sources of information, and targeted air reconnaissance.

Reconnaissance information often reveals that a certain individual would be in a certain place at a certain time. This was a crucial difference to previous attacks, which had, almost exclusively, been directed against targets catalogued on target lists defined by the CIA and JSOC[38]. The most spectacular counter terrorism operations against the leading cadre of ISIS were achieved by the use of armed drones. According to Markus Reisner, American UCAVs killed three ISIS flag bearers; Abdul Rahman Mustafa al-Kaduli, Abu al-Hija, and Abu Omar al-Schischani in 2016.

In August 2016, the USA reported the death of Abu Muhammad al-Adnani, a high-ranking ISIS founding member and its head of communications[39]. The latter was equally strike by US drone. For the first time, in summer 2016, the US government published extracts from the *Presidential Policy Guidance* (PPG): Procedures for Approving Direct Action Against Terrorist Targets Located Outside the United States and Areas of Active Hostilities. There are certain conditions which must be considered before targeted killing by drone;

---

37 European Parliament, Directorate-General for External Policies - Policy Department (ed.), 'Human Rights Implications of the Usage of Drones and Unmanned Robots in Warfare', (Brussels, 2013), p. 34.

38 Greg Miller, 'US citizen in CIA's cross hairs', (January 31, 2010), http://articles.latimes.com/ 2010/jan/31/world/la-fg-cia-awlaki31-2010jan31.

39 ibid

1. Near certainty that the terrorist target is present[40]

2. Near certainty that noncombatants will not be injured or killed

3. Assessment that the relevant governmental authorities in the country where action is contemplated cannot or will not effectively address the threat to U.S. persons

4. Assessment that capture is not feasible at the time of the operation

5. Assessment that no other reasonable alternatives exist to effectively address the threat to U.S. persons

This publication makes clear that the US government must have, by degrees, become aware that it is acting in a grey area as far as international law is concerned. The publication of the PPG could thus be understood as a first step of the USA towards greater transparency in drone warfare.

The proliferation of drones in technological era

The USA, Israel, and Great Britain were considered to be the most advanced states as regards the use of UAVs. But with recent events around the world this narrative does not longer hold, with the emergence of new actors. Though countries like France, but also Italy and Morocco, are already using American-produced drones. The Italian 32° Stormo Armando Boetto stationed in Amendola has operated RQ-1/MQ-1 Predator UAVs since 2002[41].

---

40 https://www.justsecurity.org/31764/governments-treatment-civilian-casualties-counterterrorism-operations/

41 Ibid

Source: image of RQ-1/MQ-1 adapted from defense update[42]

Italian Air Force has been using their MQ-1 Predator against ISIS[43]. France uses, inter alia, EADS Harfang MALE UAVs[44]. and also the MQ-9 Reaper, which has been used in Mali.

In Afghanistan, Germany used Heron MALE UAVs. However, Turkish armed forces' TAI Anka MALE UAV was both developed and produced domestically. Russia and China are increasingly changing the narrative of drone warfare. China's armed forces, have several drones like the CH-4 MALE UAVs and Soar Dragon HALE.

Ukrainian forces in the Donbass allegedly captured drones produced in Russia (For post and Orlan-10) and has equally been using drones since 2015[45]. Meanwhile, in 2015, the

---

42 https://defense-update.com/20050601_predator.html

43 Darren Boyle, 'La dolce obliteration: Italian air force release detailed surveillance footage showing Predator drone attacks on ISIS terrorists in Iraq', (December 11, 2015) http://www.dailymail.co.uk/news/article-3355747/La-dolce-obliteration-Italian-air-force-releasedetailed-surveillance-footage-showing-Predator-drone-attacks-ISIS-terrorists-Iraq.html.

44 Darren Boyle, 'La dolce obliteration: Italian air force release detailed surveillance footage showing Predator drone attacks on ISIS terrorists in Iraq', (December 11, 2015) http://www.dailymail.co.uk/news/article-3355747/La-dolce-obliteration-Italian-air-force-release-detailed-surveillance-footage-showing-Predator-drone-attacks-ISIS-terrorists-Iraq.html.

45 Farhan Bokhari, 'Pakistan claims first airstrike with indigenous UAV', (2015) 52 IHS Jane's Defence Weekly, Issue 37, p. 5. – The development of the Burraq

Pakistani Armed Forces announced the first successful launch of Barq air-to-ground missiles from a Burraq UAV[46]. The missiles allegedly killed three Taliban fighters in the border area between Pakistan and Afghanistan.

Iran drones are increasingly making headlines in Europe. The Iranian Shahed 129 UAV was first presented to the public in 2012[47]. The following year a video exposed a Shahed 129 launching an air-to-ground missile.

In 2015, Iraq successfully used armed Chinese CH-4B UAVs against ISIS[48]. Apart from Iraq, Egypt and Nigeria also possess this Chinese UAV type. This is another striking example of the increasing export market for drone systems of various types and sizes. It is, therefore only a matter of time until insurgent or terrorist movements in Africa own potent, unmanned systems. Since 2012, drones of various types have already been used - verifiably and repeatedly by, for example, Hamas and Hezbollah over Israel, by ISIS over Iraq and Syria, and by pro-Russian separatists in eastern Ukraine.

In 2012, Hezbollah successfully launched an Iranian Shahed-129 MALE UAV in Lebanon and flew it over Israeli territory. Only there was it possible for Israeli fighter jets to shoot it down[49]. The use of such a system by Hezbollah

---

UAV by the Pakistani armed forces was probably supported by China, as the system is very similar to the Chinese CH-3 and CH-4 UAVs. Apart from this, Pakistan also possesses the Shahpar UAV, which, according to the armed forces, can also be armed.

46 https://www.ndtv.com/world-news/pakistan-armed-drone-kills-3-in-first-attack-military-1214997

47 ibid

48 https://viennalawreview.com/index.php/vlr/article/view/52/25

49 An RQ-1 Predator had already been downed by an Iraqi MiG-25 in 2002 - the first time a US drone had been shot down. In November 2012, two Iranian Su-25 intercepted a US drone over the Persian Gulf. On 17 March 2015, an MQ-1 Predator, used as part of Operation Inherent Resolve was shot down by a

came as a nasty surprise to the Israeli Defense Forces (IDF). Two years later, during the IDF operation Protective Edge in the Gaza Strip, Hamas successfully launched a number of drones[50].

In the autumn of 2016, the first reports about drones used by the ISIS and the Taliban appeared. Given these developments, it must be assumed that in future, an increasing number of states and non-state actors will use drones for their purposes.

The use of drone by transnational actors

Drones have for some time been used by regular armed forces on Africa's battlefields, such as in Ethiopia and Mali. But now they are increasingly being deployed by terrorists – sparking a global sense of urgency.

The United Nations (UN) Security Council Counter-Terrorism Committee hosted a special meeting in India on countering the use of new technologies for terrorism. Drones or unmanned aerial systems (UAS) have been identified as one of the key terrorist threats by the meeting's organisers. Other risks are disinformation, the misuse of social media, and new payment technologies used by violent extremists. Drones are by and large a force for good, for example in delivering medicines to hard-to-reach parts of Africa. But their widespread availability, increased range and growing sophistication in terms of payload (what they can carry) have seen an expansion in their applications.

Syrian SAM-air defence battery over the Syrian province of Latakia; cf: Missy RYAN, 'U.S. drone believed shot down in Syria ventured into new area, official says', (March 19, 2015). https://www.washingtonpost.com/world/national-security/us-drone-believed-shot-down-in-syria-ventured-into-new-area-official-says/2015/03/19/891a3d08-ce5d-11e4-a2a7-9517a3a70506_story.html.

50 Bregman, 'Israel's Wars', p. 326. This was the first time a drone was brought down by a Patriot air defence system.

According to Allen (2022), hobbyist drone market has grown rapidly, with global sales increasing from $14 billion in 2018 to a projected $43 billion in 2024, according to Drone Industry Insights[51]. South Africa represents the biggest market in Africa, particularly for aerial technology used in the mining and agricultural sectors. This democratization of relatively affordable technology means that UAS can be used for nefarious ends both in wartime and peace.

The Ukraine-Russian war has underscored the significance of the new drone battlespace with an arms race in production and acquisition underway. But drones can also be bought, adapted and used to disrupt critical infrastructure such as airports, energy plants and communications networks.

As African governments assess the risks of cyber attacks on critical infrastructure such as on Transnet in South Africa in 2021, they should also consider the unintended consequences of drone proliferation (Allen, 2022). The continent has yet to witness a major installation being targeted by a UAS. There is growing evidence of drones being weaponized by violent extremists and transnational criminal networks, either as a surveillance tool or as part of their intelligence and reconnaissance operations. As ISS previously reported, armed groups such as al-Shabaab in Somalia and insurgents in the Democratic Republic of the Congo and Mozambique are applying the technology in combat.

---

51 Weaponised drones – the latest tech threat to reach Africa. As evidence grows of drones being used by terrorists and other criminals, governments should consider regulating the industry.by Karen Allen https://issafrica.org/iss-today/weaponised-drones-the-latest-tech-threat-to-reach-africa/

Al Shabaab use drone for reconnaissance and attack Somali government forces (Photo adapted from Hiiraan Online platform[52])

Fighters being trained on how to weaponize drones (Schmersahl, 2018)[53].

<hr>

52 https://www.hiiraan.com/news4/2022/Sept/187690/us_al_shabaab_has_introduced_drones_to_their_insurgency.aspx

53 Schmersahl, R. (2018) research on Fifty Feet Above The Wall: Cartel Drones In The U.S.–Mexico Border Zone Airspace, And What To Do About Them. MASTER OF ARTS IN SECURITY STUDIES from the NAVAL POSTGRADUATE SCHOOL March 2018. Also read; Stalinsky and Sosnow, "A Decade of Jihadi Organizations' Use of Drones – From Early Experiments by Hizbullah, Hamas, And Al-Qaeda to Emerging National Security Crisis for The West as ISIS Launches First Attack Drones."

UN Security Council Resolution 2617 recognizes the increasing misuse of UAS globally, including 'the misuse of unmanned aerial systems by terrorists to conduct attacks against, and incursions into, restricted commercial and government infrastructure and public places.' Council members have been urged to 'balance fostering innovation' while 'preventing the misuse of UAS.'

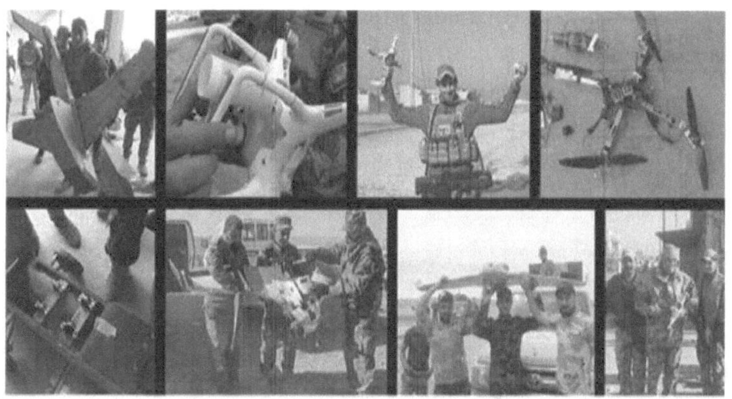

ISIS use an assortment of drones for surveillance and targeted attacks[54]

UN Office of Counter-Terrorism has developed a good practice guide on protecting vulnerable targets from drone attacks, knowing that commercial or hobbyist drones are being shaped into weapons[55]. 3D printing technology also opens up the prospect of spare parts being rapidly manufactured by extremists. While countries such as South Africa may not consider themselves at risk of an imminent terrorist attack, industry insiders worry about economic terrorism – the destabilization of essential utilities or other state services.

---

54 Ben Watson, "The Drones of ISIS," Defense One, January 12, 2017, http://www.defenseone.com/ technology/2017/01/drones-isis/134542/.

55 https://www.un.org/counterterrorism/sites/www.un.org.counterterrorism/files/2118451e-vt-mod5-unmanned_aircraft_systems_final-web.pdf

Kim James, an executive member of the Commercial Unmanned Aircraft Association of Southern Africa, confirms that crime syndicates use 'narco drones' in South Africa for basic reconnaissance and to distribute drugs. A similar tactic is seen in Colombia to evade border security measures. The prospect of drones being used to target cash-in-transit vehicles is a possibility. New regulations won't prevent the nefarious uses of drone technology, but early warning signals are necessary. They could, for example, locate suspect drones or flag the delivery of bulk purchases of hobbyist drones close to potential targets. Iraq and Syria in 2016 received consignments of hobbyist drones which were transited across the border.

13 pounds of crystal meth smuggled out of Mexico using drone (Schmersahl, 2018)[56]

---

56 "Man Smuggled 13 Pounds of Meth from Mexico Using a Drone," NBC News, August 19, 2017, https://www.nbcnews.com/news/us-news/man-smuggled-13-pounds-meth-mexico-using-drone-n794146.

Profiling the DJI Matrice 600 Pro and DJI Spreading Wings S900

A- DJI Matrice 600 Pro

Capabilities	Limitations
<ul><li>Price USD 4,999</li><li>Max recommended takeoff weight 15.5 kg (~34 lbs.)</li><li>Hover time 16 min w/ 6 kg payload (13 lbs.)</li><li>Max Speed 40 mph/65 mph no wind</li><li>Folding propeller, portable</li></ul>	<ul><li>Short battery life, as payloads increase in weight-max battery life decreases</li><li>Carry small payloads</li><li>Controller transmission max range 5 km (3.1 miles)</li><li>tested in unobstructed line of sight areas;</li><li>controller range, not a factor if the drone is capable of satellite or GPS communication (autonomous flight), limiting range factor becomes fuel or battery capacity in this case.</li></ul>

Source: Schmersahl (2018)

B- DJI Spreading Wings S900

Capabilities	Limitations
<ul><li>Price USD $1,199</li><li>Max takeoff weight 8.2kg (18 lbs.)</li><li>Hover time 15–18 min w/ 6.8kg payload (15 lbs.)</li><li>Max Speed 35 mph</li><li>Folding propeller, portable</li></ul>	<ul><li>Short battery life, takeoff weight increases-max battery life decreases.</li><li>Transport small payloads per shipment compared to trucks, cars, tunnels, submersibles</li><li>Unable to fly in high winds or rain (bad weather)</li><li>Unencrypted radio frequency controller</li></ul>

Source: Schmersahl (2018)

Audrey Kurth Cronin observed in her book ***Power to the People: How Open Technological Innovation is Arming Tomorrow's Terrorists***, 'the most common type of drone used by Islamic State was the DJI phantom, purchasable on Amazon.com for as little as 450 USD.' Export controls for such dual use technologies may also be an avenue for policymakers to consider.

Regulations require enforcement. Given the broad applications of drones, it will need an approach in which government departments coordinate their responses. In South Africa, the Commercial Unmanned Aircraft

Association of Southern Africa initiated proposals with the Department for Economic Development for a registration and accreditation process that protects the public but doesn't harm business.

Technical fixes and alerts including how to identify potentially dangerous drones, are also being developed by the private sector with a focus on big installations such as mines, pipelines, prisons, airports etc. This raises questions of who is legally permitted to intercept a drone, and of state sovereignty and international law. UN Security Council Counter-Terrorism Committee meeting reviewed some policies not to hamper the legitimate use of drones which is transforming business, agriculture, humanitarian relief and medicine in Africa. The continent is equally vulnerable to the taste of weaponized drones by militaries and insurgents.

Worldwide, the use of drones by state and non-state actors has been growing exponentially, as they are seen as efficient and relatively cheap aircraft. are deployed to gather intelligence and surveillance with the goal of tracking, 3 They detecting and identifying vehicles and people in a wide area. This information can be used to determine who or what will be attacked.

Drones are also used in circumstances that are too dangerous or difficult for fighter jets, helicopters or ground vehicles. In these cases, drones can gather intelligence in risky areas, and carry out strikes if they are armed. Drones can also support other military vehicles and aircraft in attacks that are beyond their visual range, or provide support to enable more precise strikes. Thus, a drone is an aircraft that supports military operations by monitoring and attacking threats across wide spaces, while reducing the risks for the user.

There are various types of military drones, which come in all shapes and sizes. **The North Atlantic Treaty Organization** (NATO) divides them broadly into three classes.

Class I drones are small drones, have a maximum endurance of three hours, are launched by hand or hand rail and can be operated from a maximum distance of 80 kilometers. Some of these drones are smaller than a human hand.

Class II drones, also called 'tactical' drones, can fly for a maximum of 10 hours, often need a small runway for launching and have a range of 100-200 kilometers. These drones can be equipped with infrared sensors and lasers for targeting. Some class II drones can be armed as well[57].

Class III drones, called 'medium-altitude long-endurance' (MALE) or 'high-altitude long-endurance' (HALE) drones, have an endurance of up to 24 hours or more, need a runway and have a top speed of 300 kilometers per hour or more. Some can be operated from a distance of thousands of kilometers through satellite support. Most of these drones are able to carry armaments and some can be used in 'suicide' mode, turning them into loitering munitions. The infrastructure of drones includes test sites, training grounds and drone bases, which can have runways, hangars, command and control stations, communication equipment and training ranges.

---

57 https://paxforpeace.nl/media/download/PAX_remote_horizons_FIN_ lowres.pdf

Chapter Two

The Menace Of The Exploitation Of Military Drones

With the emergence of military drones in warfare, experts have voiced serious criticisms of drone deployment in relation to international humanitarian law, human rights, international conventions and protocols on conflict and counter-terrorism. Firstly, experts argue that the use of drones equally leads to the use of lethal force and contributes to conflict escalation. The cost of drones is relatively low and it reduce military casualties but increase that of civilians. The use of drones as a counter-terrorism and counter insurgency option ignites targeted killings by armed drones, as detaining or arresting suspects will necessitate a long procedure for information for further security measures.

Secondly, drones are effective in counter-terrorism operations because of the precision of the target. Drone strikes are more precise compared with using 'dumb' munitions. However, human error is inevitable and usually results in civilian casualties when drones are used in coordinated attacks. The targets of attacks can be derived from networks of informants and data gathered by drones. The coordination and analysis of intelligence from different parties usually increase the risk of inaccurate use of the technology.

Thirdly, in so-called *'signature strikes'*[58] the targets have characteristics associated with terrorist members or combatants, such as carrying weapons, and metadata, such as gender and age, they are killed by a drone strike. The distinctions between combatants and civilians are often at the very least, ambiguous, if not non-existent. Thus, even though drones are able to strike more precisely than 'dumb' munitions, this does not mean that they do not create civilian casualties, nor that they are less prone to human error, as the teams operating them have to understand and interpret the incoming data from sensors and the underlying algorithms while working together, and to decide who is a suspect and who is not.

Misconception of Drone War in Africa

The have been proliferation of use of drones in Africa within the last decade. A sharp rise in the use of armed and unarmed drones by African and non- African states are evident in North Africa, the Sahel and the Horn of Africa. A worrisome aspect is that states are not being transparent about the deployment of drones in counter-terrorism operations. Security debates on military issues are usually restricted, particularly counter-terrorism operations.

The first wide-scale military deployment of large drones in Africa by a foreign actor was in the horn of Africa by the United States. The US deployed unarmed MQ-1 Predator drones (class III) and MQ-9 Reaper drones (class III) to gather intelligence and support artillery strikes during military missions. In 2011, the first known lethal drone attack in Africa was carried out by a US Predator drone in Somalia[59]. More so, armed and unarmed class III drones were perceived

---

58 https://www.theguardian.com/us-news/2016/jul/01/obama-continue-signature-strikes-drones-civilian-deaths

59 Ibid

in the sky in North Africa to enforce the United Nations[60] (UN) Resolution 1973 in Libya.

By 2013, American and French class III drones were acquired by Niger. Smaller drones were deployed in Chad, the Central African Republic (CAR) and Mali during security missions by the UN and the European Union. Violent non-state actors are increasingly using both small and large, armed and unarmed drones in Africa, to support their operations in North Africa, the Sahel and the Horn of Africa.

The acquisition and use of small military drones by states in North Africa and the Sahel began between 2011 and 2013, although Algeria had owned drones since 1999. Other African countries such as; Egypt, Libya, Nigeria and Tunisia also owned unarmed drones. The rise of terrorist groups like Boko Haram, made Cameroon to join other nations like Mauritania, Niger and Morocco in the quest for military drones.

National security is strictly related to information and the deployment of drones is greatly appealing for communication to the general population as to state use for national security and counter-terrorism operations. It is usually hard to verify whether drones are used in accordance with International Humanitarian Law (IHL) and International Human Rights Law (IHRL).

In armed conflict, IHL prohibits attacks that do not distinguish between military objectives and civilians or civilian objects, which also known as indiscriminate attacks. Equally, attacks must not be disproportionate, which would be the case if the expected harm to civilians or civilian objects is excessive in relation to the concrete and direct military

---

60 Richtsje Kurpershoek, Alejandra Muñoz Valdez and Wim Zwijnenburg (2021) Expanding use and proliferation of military drones in Africa https:// paxforpeace.nl/media/download/PAX_remote_horizons_FIN_lowres.pdf

advantage anticipated. Parties to the conflict are under a legal obligation to take all feasible precautions to ensure attacks are not indiscriminate or disproportionate.

It is important to note that, even in situations of armed conflict, IHRL is applicable. The right to life is a peremptory norm of international law and cannot be suspended or derogated from in times of war. Violations of IHL which may lead to the death of civilians or other protected persons, amount to a violation of the right to life. If lethal force is used outside the scope of an armed conflict, only IHRL applies, which stipulates that lethal force may only be used when strictly unavoidable to protect life. This implies that other means of self-defence must be explored beforehand and shown to be inadequate, as well as that the potential harm in the use of force does not outweigh the protective goal.

The inevitable hit on civilians during drones strikes is has also been documented about Africa. As drone operators may have mistakenly identified these civilians as armed militants or simply have been applying international law obligations inadequately. Worrisomely, governments often refuse to admit unlawful attacks, and thereby try to avoid taking responsibility for the victims of these attacks. Victims and relatives of victims of unlawful drone attacks have a right to reparations and access to information about alleged violations and investigations into such violations.

Profiling Drone Use in Africa

African and non-African states increasingly use armed and unarmed drones for counter-terrorism operations within the continent. To describe how states have been using drones in these regions, some selected countries will be discussed. The analysis shall focus on the use of drones by non-state actors and international entities in the continent. It equally explores some African countries making use of drones for counter-terrorism and counter-insurgency operations.

Non-African Actors

The United States

The U.S. Security Strategy for Sub-Saharan Africa as stated in 1995: "America's security interests in Africa are very limited. At present we have no permanent or significant military presence anywhere in Africa: We have no bases; we station no combat forces; and we homeport no ships... ultimately we see very little traditional strategic interest in Africa."[61] The 21st century changed the narrative as U.S policymakers increasingly saw Africa as "a site of valuable commercial, geopolitical, and security interests", over which the United States wanted to expose her hegemony[62]. The major change came after the 2001 attacks on the U.S.. by al-Qaeda, and the resulting 'Global War on Terror', as the US called it. As African states' borders and 'ungoverned' areas were seen as breeding grounds for terrorism, the US started to expand its military presence in Africa to counter al-Qaeda and associated armed groups.

In 2003, the US Department of Defense stated that 'it had no plans to build permanent bases, but was looking for a more flexible basing option'. As the US presence spread significantly, the US did not want "to be seen as being very much directly involved" on the continent as they were wary of being perceived as colonialist. In order to let the counter-terrorism missions in Africa play out in the shadows, the US relied heavily on the use of private military and security companies, local forces and drones instead of the deployment

---

61 Ibid

62 https://paxforpeace.nl/media/download/PAX_remote_horizons_FIN_
    lowres.pdf

of US troops[63]. Within a few years, drone bases worth millions of dollars sprang up across the African continent.

In 2007, the security activities of the US in Africa increased with the creation of the United States Africa Command (US AFRICOM)[64]. The command is responsible for all US Department of Defense operations, exercises and security cooperation on the African continent, its island nations and surrounding waters. The US wanted AFRICOM's headquarters to be based in Africa, but Germany was chosen instead because of resistance from African governments. The US operated from West African bases in Ouagadougou in Burkina Faso and Nouakchott in Mauritania for their surveillance programs to counter al-Qaeda. On the other side of the continent, the US supported the Ethiopian invasion of Somalia in 2007 by using drones to gather intelligence to counter the Islamic Courts Union and militias affiliated to them (which later became known as the al-Qaeda affiliate al-Shabaab).

U.S. drones in Somalia, Seychelles, Ethiopia and Djibouti

U.S. drone deployment began during the Obama Administration. From 2009, the U.S. partnership with Somalia will lead to creation of a base in Seychelles to gather intelligence for counter-terrorism missions. Years after, drones were armed and drone strikes were launched in Somalia. Members of Congress wrote in a letter to President Obama that the armed drone campaign had no transparency, accountability or oversight and that they were "concerned about the legal grounds for such strikes". Nevertheless, the Obama Administration continued to keep details about the drone strikes secret.

---

63 https://paxforpeace.nl/media/download/PAX_remote_horizons_FIN_lowres.pdf

64 United States Africa Command, 'About the Command', n.d. Accessed at: https://www.africom.mil/about-the-command

In 2011, the U.S. invested millions of dollars in an airfield in Arba Minch in Ethiopia for a drone base for MQ-9 Reaper drones (class III) to collect surveillance data on al-Shabaab[65]. As the base steadily turned into a key hub for counter-terrorism operations in Somalia, the US Air Force announced that the drone flights would "continue as long as the government of Ethiopia welcomes our cooperation on these varied security programs." In 2015, the base was closed down, but the US was vague about why it had stopped the drone deployments from Arba Minch.

The drone base in Ethiopia was later closed since[66] the Central Intelligence Agency (CIA) used a drone base in Mogadishu, the capital of Somalia[67]. US military intelligence agents were also involved in the counter-terrorism programme in Mogadishu. There are a few reports about how targets selection was done in Somalia, but its drone campaigns have been less transparent than the drone campaigns of the U.S. Department of Defense. For example, a New York Times article reported that in 2012, Obama was having weekly meetings called '*Terror Tuesday*', in which it was decided who in Somalia (and in other regions) should be added to the *Joint Prioritized Target List*, better known as the military's '*kill list*'[68]. The U.S. used an airbase at the Baledogle Airfield for drone operations[69].

---

65 https://paxforpeace.nl/media/download/PAX_remote_horizons_FIN_lowres.pdf

66 Ibid

67 Airwars, 'Somalia: Reported US covert actions: 2001-2016', n.d. Accessed at: https://airwars.org/archives/bij-drone-war/drone-war/data/somalia-reported-us-covert-actions-2001-2017.

68   S. Shane & J. Becker, 'Secret 'Kill List' Proves a Test of Obama's Principles and Will', The New York Times, 29 May 2012. Accessed at: https://www.nytimes.com/2012/05/29/world/obamas-leadership-in-war-on-al-qaeda.html

69 https://paxforpeace.nl/media/download/PAX_remote_horizons_FIN_lowres.pdf

In 2012, the Obama Administration reversed the 1995 strategy, adopting a new 'Strategy Toward Sub-Saharan Africa', with the stance that "Africa is more important than ever to the security and prosperity of the international community, and to the United States in particular"[70]. The new strategy was to adapt to new wave of terrorism, and the need to advance security cooperation with African countries and regional organizations through low-cost, small-footprint operations. The synergy between the U.S. and some African countries led to the tracking, apprehension, prosecution, and incarceration of terrorists. The U.S. Global Counterterrorism Forum (GCTF), which was launched in 2011 to address 21st-century terrorism united counter-terrorism coordinators, prosecutors, judges, police, border control and prison officials under a single banner.

The new strategy equally made the U.S. Department of Defense to expand its counter-terrorism missions in Africa by building and expanding drone bases. In East Africa, the Camp Lemonnier drone base in Djibouti was a supplement to the drone bases in the Seychelles and Ethiopia. In 2012, the US deployed ten Predator drones, four Reaper drones and several manned aircraft in their missions. It was revealed that an average of 16 drones and four fighters were taking off and landing at the *Camp Lemonnier* base daily[71] which remains crucial to U.S. military operations.

The U.S. Air Force operations in Djibouti paved the way for the creation of a new drone base in 2013 at Chabelly Airfield[72].

---

70 B. Obama, White House, 2012, 'U.S. Strategy Toward Sub-Saharan Africa', p. 3. Accessed at: https://2009-2017.state.gov/documents/organization/209377.pdf

71 N. Turse, 'The stealth expansion of a secret U.S. drone base in Africa', The Intercept, 21 October 2015. Accessed at: https://theintercept. com/2015/10/21/stealth-expansion-of-secret-us-drone-base-in-africa/

72 M. McCord, 25 June 2015, 'Military Construction, Navy Reprogramming Request', Department of Defense United States of America. Accessed at:https://

Drones based at the airfield cover Yemen, south-west Saudi Arabia, Somalia, Ethiopia and southern Egypt. The Pentagon out pinned that the airfield would only be used temporarily, for no more than two years. However, in 2014, however, the U.S. and Djibouti signed a long-term contract for the base.

In 2017, the U.S. reviewed the rules aimed at preventing civilian casualties for counterterrorism strikes in Somalia[73]. The new guidelines were similar to war-zone targeting rules, which allowed the U.S. to engage targets easier. Since then, AFRICOM has increased the number of airstrikes. An investigative report by Amnesty International shows that in 2017 and 2018, U.S. drone strikes in Somalia registered several casualties, including children, and might have violated IHL[74]. AFRICOM refuted the allegations but did not conduct thorough, transparent investigations into the allegations[75].

US drones used in the Maghreb

In 2011, armed MQ-1 Predator drones were acquired by Libya from the U.S. to support the NATO led intervention to implement the UN Security Council Resolution 1973, which consisted of establishing a no-fly zone over Libya to end the violence and attacks on Libyan civilians (Sims & Bergen, 2018, pp. 16, 123). The U.S. supported Libyan rebel forces in the

---

comptroller.defense.gov/Portals/45/Documents/execution/reprogramming/fy2015/milcon/15-10_MC_May_2015_Request.pdf

73 C. Savage & E. Schmitt, 'Trump Eases Combat Rules in Somalia Intended to Protect Civilians', The New York Times, 30 March 2017. Accessed at: https://www.nytimes.com/2017/03/30/world/africa/trump-is-said-to-ease-combat-rules-in-somalia-designed-to-protect-civilians.html

74 Somalia: Conflict Exacerbateshuman Right Violations And Abusesamnesty InternationalSubmission ForTheun Universal Periodic Review – 38th session Of The UPR Working Group, May 2021published November2020. https://www.amnesty.org/en/wp-content/uploads/2021/05/AFR5233152020ENGLISH.pdf

75 Ibid

intervention with an aggressive air campaign[76]. There was no diplomacy with the rebels, which led to misunderstandings of the with the 'gamers'. This laid the foundation for the post-war power struggle in Libya. The U.S. counter-terrorism strategy and synergy with Africa still continued after her intervention in Libya.

In 2016, the Tunisian government approved that the U.S. base its own unarmed Reaper drones in the country to gather intelligence on the Islamic State in Libya after the U.S. pressed the Tunisian government in secret (Richtsje Kurpershoek, Alejandra Muñoz Valdez and Wim Zwijnenburg, 2021). In return, the U.S. would share intelligence gathered by the drones with Tunisia to support their counter-terrorism operations within the country and their border security. The negotiations took place behind closed doors as the U.S. was worried that Tunisia would otherwise pull out of the deal if the government was publicly associated with an outside military power[77]. This was likely as frustration had grown among the Tunisian population with the post-revolutionary governments[78].

The U.S.-Tunisia military cooperation was broken because of the fear that, it will encourage militants to cross the border into Tunisia and link her to the U.S. military operations in Libya (Richtsje Kurpershoek, Alejandra Muñoz Valdez and Wim Zwijnenburg, 2021). The establishment of a base in Tunisia was critical to the U.S. as drones operated from Niger and Djibouti are further away from populous areas in Libya and drone flights taking off from Sigonella in Italy are often cancelled due to weather-related issues. Therefore, drones

---

76 Obama's Libya Debacle: How a Well-Meaning Intervention Ended in Failure (pp. 66-70, 71-77) Alan J. Kuperman https://www.jstor.org/stable/24483483

77 Ibid

78 https://www.arab-reform.net/publication/tunisias-parliament-a-series-of-post-revolutionary-frustrations/

flying from Tunisia have more time to gather intelligence in the region. At the end of 2016, the U.S. stated that it had conducted 495 airstrikes in Libya, of which 60 per cent were conducted with Reaper drones[79].

In 2017, several controversies emerge among American civilians about the military operation in Libya. President Donald Trump said that he did not see a U.S. role in Libya, but did see a "role in getting rid of ISIS"[80]. He further reiterated that the U.S. had a "continued commitment" in Libya to defeat jihadists. The U.S. launched at least eight airstrikes in Libya in 2017[81], though the government initially reported just four strikes as of 2018.

U.S. drones in Cameroon

U.S. has several drone bases in the Sahel region, of which Salak in Cameroon, near the northern border region between Nigeria and Chad, the U.S. extended a military base in 2013[82]. In mid-2015, Cameroon military acquired from U.S. six ScanEagle surveillance drones (Class I) at Salak and built an additional air base in Garoua for unarmed Predator drones in order to eradicate Boko Haram[83]. Captain Jennifer

---

79 S. Spittaels, N. Abou-Khalil, K. Bouhou, M. Kartas, D. McFarland & P. Servia, United Nations Security Council, 1 June 2017, 'Final report of the Panel of Experts on Libya established pursuant to resolution 1973 (2011)', p. 40. Accessed at: https://undocs.org/S/2017/466 Sims & Bergen, 2018, p. 36.

80 https://it.usembassy.gov/remarks-president-trump-prime-minister-gentiloni-italy-joint-press-conference/

81 https://www.newamerica.org/international-security/reports/airstrikes-and-civilian-casualties-libya/the-us-counterterrorism-war-and-libya/

82 R. Trafford & N. Turse, 'Cameroonian troops tortured and killed prisoners at base used for U.S. drone surveillance', The Intercept, 20 July 2017. Accessed at: https://theintercept.com/2017/07/20/cameroonian-troops-tortured-and-killed-prisoners-at-base-used-for-u-s-drone-sur-veillance/

83 D. Gettinger, The Center for the Study of the Drone, 'The American drone base in Cameroon', 21 February 2016. Accessed at: https://dronecenter.bard.edu/drone-base-cameroon/

Dyrcz, spokesperson for AFRICOM stated that, the Salak airfield was an important hub for security assistance for Cameroonian forces[84].

Scan Eagle surveillance drones given by U.S. to Cameroon military[85]

According to a report by The Intercept in 2017, the Salak base was not only used for U.S. security operations, discriminate violation of human rights. The report revealed that, most prisoners, of who were often Muslim and members of the Kanuri ethnic minority, tortured by the Cameroonian military[86]. The report equally contradicted the fact that most detainees were Boko Haram fighters, but instead ordinary people arrested on being aspirants of Boko Haram.

D. Leveille, The World, 'Can the US' new drone base in Cameroon help fight Boko Haram?', 1 March 2016. Accessed at: https://www.pri.org/stories/2016-03-01/can-us-new-drone-base-cameroon-help-fight-boko-haram

84 https://theintercept.com/2017/07/20/cameroonian-troops-tortured-and-killed-prisoners-at-base-used-for-u-s-drone-surveillance/

85 https://www.aerocontact.com/salon-aeronautique-virtuel/produit/327-drone-scaneagle

86 https://theintercept.com/2017/07/20/cameroonian-troops-tortured-and-killed-prisoners-at-base-used-for-u-s-drone-surveillance/

In 2007, the U.S. State Department's Bureau of Democracy, Human Rights and Labor reported the torture at Salak[87]. In 2016, Human Rights Report by the Department of State declared people were tortured at the Salak base, citing an Amnesty International report[88].

In 2017, Amnesty International published a new report about the torture at the base, revealing that detainees could see Americans from their cells[89]. Amnesty advocacy was for thorough, independent and impartial investigations[90]. Given the wide availability of the reports, AFRICOM's claim that it did not receive reports of human rights violations by Cameroonian forces in Salak is difficult to comprehend[91].

Later, after The Intercept and Forensic Architecture (2017) carried out additional investigations into the torture practices, AFRICOM said it would "conduct a more informal, fact-gathering inquiry in order to determine whether further investigation is warranted"[92]. AFRICOM was indifferent about the report of the latter and created several opinions on civil-military relations based on the findings of the investigation would be published.

---

87 Pentagon Denies Knowledge of Cameroon Base Abuses — Despite Being Aware of Reports of Torture. https://theintercept.com/2017/07/31/pentagon-cameroon-torture-salak-state-department/

88 Ibid

89 Richtsje Kurpershoek, Alejandra Muñoz Valdez and Wim Zwijnenburg 2021 Remote Horizons Expanding use and proliferation of military drones in Africa

90 Turse & Trafford, 31 July 2017. Cameroon's secret torture chambers: Human rights violations and war crimes in the fight against Boko Haram (2017). Amnesty International, 1-73. https://www.amnesty.org/en/documents/afr17/6536/2017/en/

91 Ibid

92 Ibid

France

French interests in Africa are linked to the colonial experience. France's reliance on natural resources on the African continent and the migration from African states to Europe. After the French colonial period in Africa ended in the 1960s, France continued to see Africa as part of its sphere of influence. In 2013, the French Ministry of Defence reiterated that, the "Sahel, from Mauritania to the Horn of Africa, together with part of sub-Saharan Africa, are [...] regions of priority interest for France due to a common history"[93]. France has also been reliant on mineral extractions in the Sahel, such as uranium, which is vital for the country's energy production.

Furthermore, since the 1990s, French secret services have monitored and countered threats, such as attacks and kidnappings, against French citizens in Africa (Carayol, 2020). France, like other European countries, has also constructed migration to its homeland as a security threat. She assumes the migration is caused by instability in African regions. With a military intervention consisting of surveillance and policing, France tries to contain migration from Africa to Europe.

The first French drones that flew in Africa in the late 2000s were to support the European Union Force Chad mission. The tactical CL-289 drones[94] (class II) were used in almost 80 missions.

---

93 Transatlantic Security from the Sahel to the Horn of Africa. IAI Research Papers https://www.iai.it/sites/default/files/iairp_12.pdf

94 CL-289 was developed as a tri-national project between Canada, France and Germany. Bombardier Inc and the Canadair Group of Canada were the system leaders and Dornier GmbH (an EADS company) the prime contractor. The CL-289 reconnaissance system is an unmanned airborne reconnaissance vehicle for use at corps and divisional level.

France started deploying MALE drones in Africa from 2011(Richtsje Kurpershoek, Alejandra Muñoz Valdez and Wim Zwijnenburg, 2021). The MALE Harfang drones (class III) were used during the NATO-led intervention in Libya to gather intelligence and for reconnaissance, but were based at Sigonella, Italy.

In 2013, France launched *Operation Serval*[95] in Mali to fight suspected 'terrorists' and restore Mali's territorial integrity. In order to get the support of the French population for the operation, the French government argued that the operation was essential for the security of France. During Operation Serval, France used class I drones, such as the French Survey Copters and Cassidian DRACs, and Harfang drones in Mali to gather intelligence which they posed it was unique.

The challenges of the *Operation Serval*, made French Minister of Defense Jean-Yves Le Drian to pounded on future strategy[96]. A few months later, an urgent order was placed through the US Foreign Military Sales programme for two unarmed MQ-9 Reaper drones, which would be deployed in Mali in January 2014.

When the military programme for 2014-2019 was adopted, France acquire 12 class III drones before 2019 and possess 30 class II drones by 2025[97] for counter terrorism operation. The class III drones, stationed at the US base in Niamey in

---

95 On August 1, 2014, Operation Serval becomes Operation Barkhane. https://www.francetvinfo.fr/monde/afrique/mali/guerre-au-mali/mali-serval-barkhane-on-vous-resume-neuf-ans-d-engagement-militaire-francais-au-sahel-en-dix-dates-cles_4966341.html

96 J. Le Drian, 'Pourquoi l'armée française a un besoin urgent de drones', Les Echos, 31 May 2013. Accessed at: https://www.lesechos.fr/2013/05/pourquoi-larmee-francaise-a-un-besoin-urgent-de-drones-1097785

97 Richtsje Kurpershoek, Alejandra Muñoz Valdez and Wim Zwijnenburg 2021 Remote Horizons Expanding use and proliferation of military drones in Africa

Niger, were used to gather intelligence in-theatre military operations, including acquiring enemy targets on the ground, and to help other armed aircraft with targeting through the use of laser sensors.

In August 2014, Operation Serval was replaced by the current counter-terrorism mission, **Barkhane**, which has been operating in Burkina Faso, Chad, Mali, Mauritania and Niger[98]. The mission began with a 3,000 strong force, including two Reaper drones and one Harfang drone[99]. The emphasis in the mission lies on the capacity to operate fast and flexibly, while having a light footprint[100]. The deployment of drones helps achieve this.

Hence in 2015, a third Reaper was equally operated by France in Niamey as well. As the military perceived the use of drones to be a success in gathering surveillance and intelligence for their counter-terrorism operations, France announced in 2017 that they had decided to arm their drones in the future. Worryingly however, neither France nor the Europe Union have formulated a clear policy on how and when they would use the armed drones.

France carried out its first drone strike in Mali in December 2019, only two days after the army finished testing drones for armed operations. In the operation, in which helicopters and ground troops were deployed as well, 40 "terrorists" were "neutralized"[101]. Ten days later, nine terrorists were "put out

---

98 'François Hollande's African adventures', The Economist, 21 July 2014. Accessed at: https://www.economist.com/europe/2014/07/21/francois-hollandes-african-adventures

99 Ibid

100 Whitlock, 1 September 2014. The Economist, 21 July 2014. Accessed at: https://www.economist.com/europe/2014/07/21/francois-hollandes-african-adventures

101 Protecting vulnerable targets from terrorist attacks involving unmanned aircraft systems (UAS) GOOD PRACTICES GUIDESpecialized module.

of action" with the aid of a combat helicopter and armed Reaper drone.

In January 2020, 35 militants and 23 motorcycles were "neutralized" by combat helicopters and an armed drone[102]. The French military announced 50 militants were neutralized,30 motorcycles and two pickup trucks destroyed in Mali with the help of a Reaper drone, Mirage 2000 airstrikes and combat helicopters[103].

A French Reaper drone armed with 2 GBU-12 bombs at the operation Barkhane's military base in Niamey, on December 15, 2019[104].

---

https://www.un.org/counterterrorism/sites/www.un.org.counterterrorism/files/2118451e-vt-mod5-unmanned_aircraft_systems_final-web.pdf

102 Ministère des Armées, 'Barkhane : Opérations ponctuelles au Mali', 29 January 2020. Accessed at: https://www.defense.gouv.fr/operations/barkhane/breves/barkhane-operations-ponctuelles-au-mali

103 Ministère des Armées, 'Barkhane : Opérations dans la région de Mopti', 20 February 2020. Accessed at: https://www.defense.gouv.fr/operations/actualites2/barkhane-operations-dans-la-region-de-mopti

104 Richtsje Kurpershoek, Alejandra Muñoz Valdez and Wim Zwijnenburg 2021 Remote Horizons Expanding use and proliferation of military drones in Africa

Most of the phrases used by the French military to justified targeted attacks are "putting terrorists out of action" and "neutralizing armed militants" instead of using the words 'killing' or 'executing'. Moreover, press releases let the public believe that there have been almost no civilian casualties in the French military operations. However, it is extremely difficult for the French military to know who the 'terrorists' are, as most jihadists hide among the populations, making everyone a potential suspect. However French news portal Media part testimonials revealed that during that military operation, several casualties were registered following an attack from a French drone.

In general, independently tracking possible civilian casualties in the Sahel remains difficult. Western journalists have to follow the instructions of the French army and do not have freedom of movement in the regions, unless they are willing to take the risk of travelling without protection. Therefore, it is extremely difficult to verify whether there are indeed no attacks on civilians, as the French government claims.

Italy

After it gave up its colony Libya in 1943, Italy retained major strategic interests in Africa. Italy relays on oil and natural gas from Libya and, like other European member states, seeks to have control over the migrants who cross the Mediterranean to come to Europe[105]. Since 2004, Italy has bought six Predator drones, and it has introduced six Reaper drones since 2010[106]. These unarmed drones are used actively

---

105 https://www.euractiv.com/section/politics/news/italy-forges-pact-on-gas-migrants-with-libya/

106 J. Drew, 'Italian delivery marks end of General Atomics RQ-1 production', FlightGlobal, 23 December 2015. Accessed at: https://www.flightglobal.com/italian-delivery-marks-end-of-general-atomics-rq-1-production/119202. article Ministero Della Difesa, 'MQ-1C Predator A+', n.d. Accessed at: http://www.aeronautica.difesa.it/mezzi/mlinea/Pagine/MQ1CPREDATORAB.

over the Mediterranean and during NATO operations for reconnaissance, surveillance and target acquisition missions.

In 2011, several African countries acquired drones. In 2015, less than 40 per cent of the population were aware that Italy deployed drones in its military missions[107]. This raises the question of accountability of the state to communicate to the public about the deployment of drones and the menace related to troops on the soil.

In 2016, the Italian population learned that the U.S. had armed the drones that were based in Italy[108]. However, Italian government refused to admit that American armed drone operations took place. Furthermore, the Italian government did not publicly declare a clear policy and legal position on the use of armed drones, despite consistent calls from European and Italian civil society organizations.

The Italian militarily intervention in Libya alongside NATO members was to implement the ***United Nations Security Council Resolution 1973***, and was done with an unarmed Reaper to gather intelligence. By the end of the year, the Reaper had transmitted 250 hours of video. During the intervention, Italy asked the US for permission to arm the drone, which it received in 2015. It remains however unclear whether Italian drones have been armed or not.

---

aspx Peruzzi, 15 August 2011. Ministero Della Difesa, 'Predator', n.d. Accessed at: https://www.difesa.it/SGD-DNA/Staff/DT/ARMAEREO/Programmi/UAV-Drone/Pagine/Predator.aspx

107 S. Cvijic, L. Klingenberg, D. Goxho & E. Knight, Open Society Foundations, 2019 'Armed drones in Europe', p. 51. Accessed at: https://www.opensocietyfoundations.org/publications/armed-drones-in-europe Istituto di Ricerche Internazionali Archivio Disarmo, 2017, 'Droni militari: Proliferazione o controllo?'. Accessed at: https://www.disarmo.org/rete/docs/5137.pdf

108 https://www.ecchr.eu/en/case/sicily-air-base-freedom-of-information-litigation-on-italys-involvement-in-us-drone-program/

Operation Mare Sicuro

In 2013, Italy began *Operation Mare Sicuro*, a surveillance and maritime security operation near the coast of Libya and in the Mediterranean, in which Predator drones were deployed[109]. The Defense Minister Mario Mauro stated that the drones could be used to identify and track boats with migrants as well. In November 2019, an Italian Reaper crashed in Tripoli, the capital of Libya, where rival groups had been fighting each other[110]. The Libyan National Army stated that they shot the Reaper down, posting photos of the wreckage on social media. Yet Italy's Ministry of Defence said that contact with the Reaper had been lost during a Mare Sicuro operation.

Operation Atlanta

In 2014, Italy deployed one of its unarmed Italian Predators in Djibouti from Chabelly Airport to support the European Union's anti-piracy mission *Operation Atlanta*[111]. However, the sphere of the operation increased, as the Italian Ministry of Defense did not officially announce its drone expansion to Djibouti. The Predator drone monitored pirates along the Somali coast and World Food Programme ships transporting goods to Somalia. Members of parliament asked the Defense

---

109 Senato Della Repubblica, 2017, 'Relazione Sullo stato della disciplina militare e sullo stato dell'organizzazione delle forze armate', p. 166.Accessed at: http://www.senato.it/service/PDF/PDFServer/DF/343378.pdf

110 T. Kington, 'Italy confirms military drone crashed in Libya', Defense News, 20 November 2019. Accessed at: https://www.defensenews.com/global/europe/2019/11/21/italy-confirms-military-drone-crashed-in-libya/#:~:text=ROME%20%E2%80%94%20An%20unarmed%20Italian%20Air,in%20the%20country's%20civil%20conflict.&text=The%20drone%20was%20%E2%80%9Cfollowing%20a,staff%20said%20in%20a%20statement .

111 Maxalb, 'Droni, marò e parà italiani contro pirati e shebab somali', Africa ExPress, 5 March 2020. Accessed at: https://www.africa-express.info/2014/09/03/droni-maro-e-para-italiani-contro-pirati-e-shabab-somali/

Minister if Italian drones were being used to support the secret US mission to counter the al-Shabaab militant group in Somalia as well, but the latter refused to respond (Richtsje Kurpershoek, Alejandra Muñoz Valdez and Wim Zwijnenburg, 2021).

United Nations

The UN has been using drones in monitoring operations since 2006. In 2006, drones were used in the EUFOR RD Congo military operation by Belgium troops in the Democratic Republic of Congo to support the UN peacekeeping mission MONUC and in Sudan after the UN Security Resolution 1706 gave a mandate "to monitor trans-border activities of armed groups along the Sudanese borders with Chad and the Central African Republic."[112]

In 2009, the UN replaced the European Union military operation in Chad and the Central African Republic in which surveillance was done by drones[113]. In 2013, the UN deployed drones in (the *United Nations Operation in Côte d'Ivoire (UNOCI)*) Côte d'Ivoire, though at the end the end, the drones were not authorized due to an improvement in the security situation[114].

---

112 Apuuli (2014) The Use of Unmanned Aerial Vehicles (Drones) in United Nations Peacekeeping: The Case of the Democratic Republic of Congo. https://www.asil.org/insights/volume/18/issue/13/use-unmanned-aerial-vehicles-drones-united-nations-peacekeeping-case

113 UN council authorizes force to replace EU in Chad by Patrick Worsnip. https://www.reuters.com/article/ozatp-chad-un-20090115-idAFJOE 50E02820090115

114 United Nations Security Council, 'Côte d'Ivoire Has Entered 'New Phase' in Consolidating Peace, But Still Faces Formidable Threats that Require Continued UN Presence, Security Council Told', 16 April 2013. Accessed at: https://www.un.org/press/en/2013/sc10973.doc.htm ; M. Nichols, 'U.N. seeks surveillance drones for Mali, shelves plans for Ivory Coast', Reuters, 12 May 2014. Accessed at: https://www.reuters.com/article/us-un-drones-ivorycoast-mali-idUSBREA4B0R720140512

In 2013, the ***Stabilization Mission in the Democratic Republic of the Congo (MONUSCO)*** did get formal approval to use drones to track movements of armed militias and document atrocities, despite general skepticism on the use of drones among UN member states[115]. Member states criticized the intelligence that drones would generate, as states feared that any intelligence collection powers on the part of the UN could lead to the loss of sovereignty of member states. Nevertheless, the UN did start expanding its use of drones after deploying them during MONUSCO, as they proved to be a useful tool in UN missions.

A panel of experts on Technology and Innovation in UN Peacekeeping stated for example in 2014 that the use of drones constituted "an indispensable source of information" and that "their use should [...] be immediately expanded" and "maximum use" should be made of smaller drones, as the "UN peacekeeping simply cannot afford to cede the information advantage to those actors in a mission area determined to undermine prospects for peace and who use the advantages of modern technology to aid their violent cause"[116].

In the Multidimensional Integrated Stabilization Mission in Mali (MINUSMA), the Netherlands deployed ScanEagle and Raven drones (class I) from 2014 to 2016 from Camp Castor in Mali for intelligence. The ScanEagles flew more than 1,000 hours. In 2015, Sweden supported Dutch military effort with Shadow (class II), Wasp (class I) and Puma (class

---

115   Karlsrud, & Rosén, 2013, pp. 2-3 D. Gilman, OCHA Policy Development and Studies Branch, 2014, 'Unmanned Aerial Vehicles in Humanitarian Response', p. 13. Accessed at:https://www.unocha.org/sites/unocha/files/Unmanned%20Aerial%20Vehicles%20in%20Humanitarian%20Response%20OCHA%20July%202014.pdf

116   Performance Peacekeeping: Final Report of the Expert Panel on Technology and Innovation in UN Peacekeeping. https://walterdorn.net/home/255-expert-panel-on-technology-and-innovation-report

I) drones from a base in Timbuktu, Mali[117]. German Heron 1 (class III) and LUNA drones (class I) were used to support MINUSMA operations[118]. One of the major challenge at the time was that, the UN lacked analysts who could interpret the data gathered by the drones.

In 2015, UN requested the South Sudanese government to allow her operate UAVs[119]. The government however dismissed all requests because they did not allow their military installations to be photographed. They equally challenged UN's request for the use of drones, for the fact that, she believe no terrorist hub exist in the country.

In 2017, the government of the Central African Republic did approve the use of drones during the United Nations Multidimensional Integrated Stabilization Mission in the Central African Republic (MINUSCA)[120] (Howard et al 2020). French tactical drones were used to locate armed groups during operation Sangaris[121].

The Acquisition of Drones by African States

Tunisia

In 2011, internal wrangling spark in Tunisia, with civilians demanding a solution for the high unemployment, food

---

117 Ibid

118 Ibid

119 South Sudan rejected UN request to deploy aerial drones: report by Radio Tamazuj - 3 Jul 2014. https://radiotamazuj.org/en/news/article/south-sudan-rejected-un-request-to-deploy-aerial-drones-report

120 Assessing the Effectiveness of the United Nations Integrated Multidimensional Stabilization Mission in the Central African Republic (MINUSCA). https://effectivepeaceops.net/wp-content/uploads/2020/10/EPON-MINUSCA-Report.pdf

121 Thierry VIRCOULON, interviewé par François Gapihan sur BFM TV. Fin de l'opération Sangaris: La Centrafrique peut-elle remercier militaires français? https://www.ifri.org/fr/espace-media/lifri-medias/fin-de-loperation-sangaris-centrafrique-remercier-militaires-francais?language=fr

inflation, corruption, lack of political freedom and poor living conditions. The ousting of President Zine El Abidine Ben Ali[122], led to the election of Moncef Marzouki as President; he acquired ScanEagle drones (class I), from the US. More so, the Tunisia secretly allowed U.S. Reaper drones to be based in her country in 2016. When the existence of the U.S. drone base was revealed to the public in October 2016, Colonel Behlhassen Oueslati refuted that U.S. drones were based in the country and used in counter-terrorism operations in Libya[123]. Defense Minister Farhat Horchani stated that, the drones were in Tunisia for training purposes and to "monitor the southern borders and detect any suspicious movements"[124]. "Tunisia is a sovereign country and will not host foreign bases," he added.

However, Tunisian President later approved American drones to fly from the Tunisian base, despite the controversial stance of Tunisian population and parliament. Notwithstanding, the commander of US AFRICOM call Tunisia "one of [their] most capable and willing partners"[125]. The Tunisian military further acquired more drones systems (class I) in 2019. In 2020, Tunisia ordered six Turkish Anka-S drones (class III) in 2020, but it was later reported that the contract was

---

122 https://www.dw.com/en/new-interim-president-takes-oath-in-tunisia/a-14768185

123 Agence Tunis Afrique Presse, 'Le ministère de la Défense nie l'existence de bases militaires américaines en Tunisie', 27 October 2016.Accessed at:https://www.tap.info.tn/fr/Portail-%C3%A0-la-Une-FR-top/8362882-le-minist%C3%A8re-de-la-d%C3%A9fense-nie

124 M. Hosenball & A. Shalal, 'U.S. using Tunisia to conduct drone operations in Libya: U.S. sources', Reuters, 26 October 2016. Accessed at:https://www.reuters.com/article/us-usa-drones-tunisia-idUSKCN12Q2PW

125 https://paxforpeace.nl/media/download/PAX_remote_horizons_FIN_lowres.pdf

cancelled because of inadequate funds[126]. One of the major characteristic of the Anka-S drone is its capability of carrying weapons.

Libya

In 2009, Ghaddafi order four Camcopter S-100 drones (class II) from Austria; but the drones were delivered in early 2011[127]. The purchase of Austria drones was to monitor the border and control migration. Though Ghaddafi used the drones however to fight insurgents[128].

In early 2011, the United Nations implemented an arms embargo against Libya, expressing "grave concern at the situation in the Libyan Arab Jamahiriya and [condemning] the violence and use of force against civilians"[129]. In March 2011, a NATO-led coalition started a military intervention was necessary in Libya to implement the *United Nations Security Council Resolution 1973*, in quest for; immediate ceasefire, end to violence and attacks against civilians, as well

126 B. E. Bekdil, 'Turkey's TAI sells six Anka-S drones to Tunisia', DefenseNews, 16 March 2020. Accessed at: https://www.defensenews.com/ unmanned/2020/03/16/turkeys-tai-sells-six-anka-s-drones-to-tunisia/L. Sariibrahimoglu, 'Roketsan chief says Tunisia interested in guided bombs for UAVs', Janes, 20 October 2020. Accessed at: https://www.janes.com/ defence-news/rokestan-chief-says-tunisia-interested-in-guided-bombs-for-uavs/

127 Stockholm Peace Research Institute, "SIPRI Arms Transfers Database," n.d. Accessed at: https://www.sipri.org/databases/armstransfers'Rot-weiß-rote Drohnen in Gaddafis Diensten', Der Standard, 1 March 2011. Accessed at: https://www.derstandard.at/story/1297819293825/ austro-kriegsmaterial-rot-weiss-rote-drohnen-in-gaddafis-diensten

128 Österreichische Drohnen für Gaddafis Regime', Die Presse, 1 March 2011. Accessed at: https://www.diepresse.com/638487/osterreichische-drohnen-fur-gaddafis-regime

129 UN Resolution 1970 imposing sanctions on Libya. https://www.voltairenet. org/article168645.html

as a no-fly zone over Libya[130]. The resolution furthermore provided necessary measures for the protection of civilians, embargo on the sale and acquisition of arms by the regime. However, in order to challenge the governing administration, a Canadian company Aeryon Labs Inc. supplying rebels with a quadcopter (class I), worth USD 120,000, to support their ground operations against Ghaddafi[131]. The small drones remained popular with citizens and certain militia brigades.

In 2014, a second civil war broke out in Libya[132]. This civil war is was fought between the Libyan National Army (LNA), led by commander-in-chief Mashal Khalifa Haftar, and the Government of National Accord (GNA), led by Fayez al-Sarray. Haftar was backed by the UAE, Egypt, Russia, Saudi Arabia, Jordan and France, while al-Sarray was supported by the UN, Italy and other Western states, Turkey and Qatar[133]. It is unlikely that the LNA and GNA operate these drones without adequate training and maintenance of these drones are complex, which must be challenging for militants. Armed groups usually use smaller drones, like the Austrian

---

130 Resolution 1973 (2011), Adopted by the Security Council at its 6498th meeting, on 17 March 2011. https://www.refworld.org/docid/4d885fc42.html

131 L. Friese, N. R. Jenzen-Jones & M. Smallwood, Armament Research Services and PAX, 2016, 'Emerging Unmanned Threats: The use ofcommercially-available UAVs by armednon-state actors', p. 48. Accessed at: https://www.academia.edu/37605935/Emerging_Unmanned_Threats_The_use_of_commercially-available_UAVs_by_armed_non-state_actors K. Hill, 'How Libyan Rebels Got A \$120,000 Micro-Drone' Forbes, 26 August 2011. Accessed at: https://www.forbes.com/sites/kashmirhill/2011/08/26/how-libyan-rebels-got-a-120000-mini-drone/#3dc4a8aa29de

132 Korotaev A., Isaev L., Shishkina A. Second Wave of the Libyan Civil War: Factors and Actors. World Economy and International Relations, 2021, vol. 65, No 3, pp. 111-119. https://doi.org/10.20542/0131-2227-2021-65-3-111-119

133 Richtsje Kurpershoek, Alejandra Muñoz Valdez and Wim Zwijnenburg 2021 Remote Horizons Expanding use and proliferation of military drones in Africa

Schiebel Camcopter S 100 drones to conduct their operation (Kurpershoek, R. et al 2021).

Bayraktar TB2 drone from Turkey acquired by Burkina Faso[134]

In 2016, the LNA was able to use at least two and possibly up to eight combat UAE Wing Loong II drones (class III)[135]. In 2019, one of the Wing Loong II drones, which was paired with five BA-7 missiles, was destroyed, while another one had been spotted near Tripoli[136]. It alleged GNA acquired Turkish Bayraktar TB2 drones (class III) in 2019, which were manufactured by Baykar Makina[137] which were destroyed by LNA forces in June 2019[138].

In 2019, the use of drones intensified in the Libyan civil war as they became the main means to conduct aerial attacks for both parties. Within a year, the LNA and affiliated forces

---

134 https://www.military.africa/2022/09/burkina-faso-buys-5-bayraktar-tb2-drones-from-turkey/

135 Ibid

136 https://paxforpeace.nl/media/download/PAX_remote_horizons_FIN_lowres.pdf

137 https://www.baykartech.com/en/uav/bayraktar-tb2/

138 Ibid

conducted about 850 drone strikes[139]. The GNA and affiliates on their part, conducted about 250 airstrikes, of which an unknown number were performed by drones[140]. Though non state actors and militia groups usually claim responsibility for attacks, in Libya even foreign nations refrain from communicating on the use of drones for attacks.

In January 2020, Turkey and Russia pushed the warring parties to declare a ceasefire, yet the war only intensified. When the coronavirus spread through the country, hospitals and civilian buildings were a target for the drones. The GNA carried out attacks near Tripoli, but the LNA claimed responsibility for taking down some drones belonging to her counterpart (Kurpershoek, R. et al 2021). The GNA declared shooting down a Wing Loong drone, operated by the UAE[141]. GNA equally revealed that Jordan sold a Chinese Wing Loong drone to the LNA,but the latter refuted[142].

Both sides not only use class III drones in their fight against each other, but also deploy smaller drones in their operations for intelligence, surveillance and reconnaissance. The LNA deploys an unknown number of Orlan-10 (class I) and Mohadjer-2 (class I) drones, while the GNA has Orbiter-3 drones (class I) (Kurpershoek, R. et al 2021).

---

139 United Nations Security Council, 15 January 2020, 'United Nations Support Mission in Libya Report of the Secretary-General', p. 4-5. Accessed at:https://unsmil.unmissions.org/sites/default/files/sg_report_to_sc_15_january_2020_eng.pdf

140 Richtsje Kurpershoek, Alejandra Muñoz Valdez and Wim Zwijnenburg 2021 Remote Horizons Expanding use and proliferation of military drones in Africa

141 Libya's GNA shoots down Wing Loong drone for Haftar's forces by Libyan Express.   https://www.libyanexpress.com/libyas-gna-shoots-down-wing-loong-drone-for-haftars-forces/

142 Libya's GNA says Jordan sold UAVs to its enemy by Jeremy Binnie. https://www.janes.com/defence-news/news-detail/update-libyas-gna-says-jordan-sold-uavs-to-its-enemy

Mali

In 2012, Mali did not only experienced the Tuareg uprising, with the seizure of northern cities by Islamist groups including Ansar Dine and al-Qaeda in the Islamic Maghreb (AQIM), and a military coup[143]. In 2013, France began to deploy drones in Mali in order to fight Islamist groups. Malians first welcome the security partnership, before some local will begin decrying certain activities of the French.

In 2016, the Malian population organized several protests against the foreign forces operating in the country[144]. The population accused the French army of going after innocent people, and added that, neither the French forces nor the Malian government provided information about the various French military operations. But Major General Patrick Bréthous told Malian journalist Baba Ahmed "we are not here to highlight the results of our operations, but rather to ensure that the armed terrorist groups no longer have any sanctuary."[145] He argued that the Malian authorities should decide whether or not to provide information about the military operations. However, the Malian authorities have sanctioned journalists who cover security issues[146] not forgetting that, criticizing the army can result in arrests on

---

143 G. Chauzal & T. Van Damme, Clingendael, 'The roots of Mali's conflict

Moving beyond the 2012 crisis', 2015. Accessed at:https://www.clingendael.org/sites/default/files/pdfs/The_roots_of_Malis_conflict.pdf

144   At least one dead in protest in north Mali against French forces by Reuters Staff. https://www.reuters.com/article/us-mali-security-idUSKCN0XF24E

145   B. Ahmed, 'Gal Patrick Bréthous (Barkhane) : au Mali, « les terroristes fuient les forces internationales »', Jeune Afrique, 29 July 2016. Accessed at: https://www.jeuneafrique.com/345701/politique/gal-patrick-brethous-barkhane-mali-terroristes-fuient-forces-internationales/

146 The safety of journalists in Mali: a daily challenge for a country in reconstruction   by   OCHA.https://reliefweb.int/report/mali/safety-journalists-mali-daily-challenge-country-reconstruction

charges of contravening standards and undermining troop morale[147].

After locals later protested in Kidal in northeast Mali, then another protested at the French embassy in Bamako in 2018[148]. The anti-French sentiment among the Malian population rose even further in 2019, after at least 41 Malian soldiers were murder in a ***military camp of Boulkessi***[149]. Conspiracy theory emerge on social networks about France was assisting the jihadists, and her inability to halt the attacks on the population, despite its sophisticated weapons and drones[150]. After a formidable coup in Mali, France was ousted from the country.

Niger

Within two decades, Niger witness three coup d'états (1996, 1999 and 2010) before the election of Majamadou Issoufou to office in 2011(Barka & Ncube, 2012)[151]. Issoufou's government took a hardline stance against terrorism and irregular migration by oriented most of her budget on defense like other African states to secure the borders. Simultaneously, Issoufou became head of the G5 Sahel counter-terrorism

---

147 UNITED NATIONS DEMOCRACY FUND (2021) POST PROJECT EVALUATIONS on Strengthening CSO Engagement with Defence Institutions to Reduce Corruption and Strengthen Accountability in Mali. https://www.un.org/democracyfund/sites/www.un.org.democracyfund/files/mali-udf-16-696-mli-final-evaluation-report_er_0.pdf

148 Protests against French forces in Mali turn deadly. https://www.france24.com/en/20160418-mali-kidal-deadly-protests-against-french-forces

149 Ahmed, 24 October 2019.

150 Denis M. Tull, "Contesting France: Rumors,Interventionand the Politics of Truthin Mali", Critique Internationale, 90(1), 2021.

151 https://www.afdb.org/sites/default/files/documents/publications/economic_brief_-_political_fragility_in_africa_are_military_coups_detat_a_never_ending_phenomenon.pdf

force and security synergy was created with France and U.S. (Kurpershoek, R. et al 2021).

US began to deploy drones in Niger to fight armed Islamists and drug traffickers began in 2013[152]. Meanwhile in 2014, U.S. established a new drone base in Agadez in Niger[153]. However, it was alledged parliament was not informed of the security trends particularly the approval for the construction of the base, although this is required by the Nigerien defense treaties[154].

Djibril Abarchi, chairman of the Nigerien Association for the Defence of Human Rights, an independent watchdog group, said "we just know there are drones; we don't know what they are doing exactly. Nothing is visible. There is no transparency in our country with military questions. No one can tell you what's going on."[155] Nigerien authorities imposed restrictions on press freedom, denied civil society demonstrations and made hundreds of arbitrary arrests (Kurpershoek, R. et al 2021) for those who opposed the U.S. drone deployment.

In 2016, Issoufou was re-elected, but population protested and terrorists exploited the events to attack. Issoufou grant U.S. permission to arm its drones, to the dismay of

---

152   Niger would welcome armed U.S. drones: foreign minister by Daniel Flynn, Abdoulaye Massalatchi. https://www.reuters.com/article/us-niger-drones/niger-would-welcome-armed-u-s-drones-foreign-minister-idUSBRE98H0PW20130918

153   U.S. military is building a $100 million drone base in Africa, The Intercept, 29 September 2016. Accessed at: https://theintercept.com/2016/09/29/u-s-military-is-building-a-100-million-drone-base-in-africa/

154   Humanitarian law manual for armed forces by International Committee of the Red Cross. 25 March 2015 https://www.icrc.org/en/document/niger-humanitarian-law-manual-armed-forces

155   Richtsje Kurpershoek, Alejandra Muñoz Valdez and Wim Zwijnenburg 2021 Remote Horizons Expanding use and proliferation of military drones in Africa

the opposition[156] which made adversaries believe foreign powers were infringement the sovereignty of their country. According to Nouhou Mahamadou "The presence of foreign bases in general and American in particular is a serious surrender of our sovereignty and a serious attack on the morale of the Nigerien military,"[157]. Amadou Roufai, a Niger administration official, revealed that citizens are afraid of casualties caused by drones strike on population or poor targeting. AFRICOM however stated that drones would only carry out strikes for self-defense purposes.

A crashed US MQ-1C Grey Eagle with Hellfire missiles that crash-landed in Niger, January 26, 2021[158].

---

156 U.S. confirms deployment of armed drones in Niger by Reuters Staff. https://www.reuters.com/article/us-usa-niger-security-drones-idUSKBN1KK18C

157 'US builds drone base in Niger, crossroads of extremism fight', Defense News, 23 April 2018. Accessed at: https://www.defensenews.com/unmanned/2018/04/23/us-builds-drone-base-in-niger-crossroads-of-extremism-fight/

158 Richtsje Kurpershoek, Alejandra Muñoz Valdez and Wim Zwijnenburg 2021 Remote Horizons Expanding use and proliferation of military drones in Africa

Most Africans consider security cooperation as a new form of colonialism, though it has help in the global war on terror even in Africa. However, some like the mayor of Dirkou, Boubakar Jerome, approved of the US drone bases as they scare people[159]. Some considered it as a source of income, while others criticized the noise caused by the drones base in Dirkou[160].

In 2019, a large demonstration broke out in Niamey[161] in which protesters requested the departure of foreign forces, as they infringed Niger's sovereignty. The protesters said that the national army should be provided with sufficient and adequate resources, so they could ensure their own security.

In 2019, Niger army expanded her asernal, but also allowed France to arm its drones. The military received three French Delair DT26X Surveillance drones (class I) to support their military missions[162]. In 2020, Niger received another batch of surveillance drones for counter terrorism operations[163].

Chad

Idriss Déby Itno has been the President of Chad since 1990 and under his reign several attempted coups and riots were recorded. In 2008, rebels entered the capital of Chad, N'Djamena, France deployed 11 CL-289 drones (class II)

---

159 https://www.nytimes.com/2018/09/09/world/africa/cia-drones-africa-military.html

160 Ibid

161 Niger: Violent clashes between protesters and police in Niamey, Oct. 29, 2017. https://crisis24.garda.com/alerts/2017/10/niger-violent-clashes-be-tween-protesters-and-police-in-niamey-oct-29?origin=fr_riskalert

162 Delair long range surveillance drones help the French Ministry of Foreign Affairs to better address counter terrorism in Niger. https://delair.aero/success-stories/delair-long-range-surveillance-drones-help-the-french-ministry-of-foreign-affairs-to-better-address-counter-terrorism-in-niger/

163 Ibid

to gather intelligence and help push back the rebels[164]. A Chadian news outlet questioned the usefulness of these drones at the time.

In 2014, Chadian news reported that the U.S. had started to deploy drones from Chad to help rescue the Chibok girls abducted by Boko Haram Nigeria (Kurpershoek, R. et al 2021). In 2019, France supported Déby again when suspected militants entered Chadian territory from Libya by deploying a Reaper drone, which destroyed around 20 pickup trucks[165]. Chad-France security synergy is undisputed, even with the present administration.

Nigeria

In 2006, Nigeria acquired Israeli Aerostar drones (class II)[166] to carry out surveillance on Boko Haram militants. The use of drone is very essential for counter terrorism operations in West Africa, particularly with the mutations of Boko Haram's modus operandi. These drones help for intelligence, reconnaissance and strike on the target.

---

164 'Des drones français au Tchad – Libération', Tchad Actuel, 28 June 2008. Accessed at : http://www.tchadactuel.com/?p=2013

165 Richtsje Kurpershoek, Alejandra Muñoz Valdez and Wim Zwijnenburg 2021 Remote Horizons Expanding use and proliferation of military drones in Africa

166 Ibid

GULMA is the first drone to be fabricated in Nigeria in 2013, for intelligence, surveillance and recognition. Image adapted from Congodiaspo.

The menace posed by Boko Haram made the government to declare a state of emergency in 2013 in the regions of Borno, Yobe and Adamawa, where Boko Haram had been fighting. In 2013, the Nigerian Air Force built their first light **GULMA drones** as well to gather intelligence during their military missions against Boko Haram[167]. The drones were not deployed for counter terrorism operations at the time (Kurpershoek, R. et al 2021).

In 2014, Nigeria authorized the US to use unarmed Predator drone in the search for 250 Nigerian schoolgirls abducted by Boko Haram[168]. Though some people in northern Nigeria began preaching conspiracy theories that, the US and other Western forces were trying to destroy Muslims and dominate

---

167 Nigeria: Gulma Drone – a Step Towards Technological Advancement. https://www.suasnews.com/2013/12/nigeria-gulma-drone-a-step-towards-technological-advancement/

168 https://paxforpeace.nl/media/download/PAX_remote_horizons_FIN_lowres.pdf

Islam (THURSTON, 2016)[169]. Civilians worried that the Nigerian government was allowing these foreign powers to take over the country.

Chinese Wing Loong II armed drones acquired by Nigerian Air Force in September 2020[170].

Nigeria purchased armed Chinese CH-3A drones (class II) which the use in military mission in Borno Province against Boko Haram[171]. The Nigerian Air Force continued to use drones in counter-terrorism operations. In 2016, the Nigerian Air Force conducted a drone strike against Boko Haram, which "destroyed" their logistics base (Kurpershoek, R. et al 2021).

---

169 https://www.brookings.edu/wp-content/uploads/2016/07/brookings-analysis-paper_alex-thurston_final_web.pdf

170 Richtsje Kurpershoek, Alejandra Muñoz Valdez and Wim Zwijnenburg 2021 Remote Horizons Expanding use and proliferation of military drones in Africa

171 Did An Armed Chinese-Made Drone Just Crash in Nigeria? CH-3 UCAVs Join War Against Boko Haram By Jeffrey Lin and P.W. Singer | Published Jan 28, 2015 6:00 PM EST. https://www.popsci.com/did-armed-chinese-made-drone-just-crash-nigeria/

In 2018, Nigeria expanded its air campaign by carrying out multiple strikes on Boko Haram in north-east Nigeria with its CH-3A drones, killing and demolished their vehicles[172]. The Nigerian Air Force also shared videos in which a drone destroys a gun truck and artillery gun belonging to Boko Haram[173]. The Nigeria Air Force developed its own surveillance drone in collaboration with Portugal, the *Tsaigumi (class I)*, in 2018[174]. The air force is working on the combat drone *Ichoku*, essential for the continuous battle against Boko Haram[175].

President Muhammadu Buhari hailed the Nigerian Air Force for the drone development stating "all necessary measures to tackle all forms of criminality across the country and to safeguard lives and property of all Nigerians"[176]. He equally tasked the air force with the mass production of Tsaigumi drones, as this could "possibly generate revenue as Nigeria's first military export product"[177].

Cameroon

In 2001, Cameroon created the Rapid Intervention Battalion (BIR), an elite force to fight armed groups in the northern

---

172 Ibid

173 Ibid

174 NAF's new Drone TSAIGUMI in Hard Strike Exercise. https://globalpatriotnews.com/nafs-new-drone-tsaigumi-in-hard-strike-exercise/?pr=146303&lang=fr

175 Nigerian Air Force explains controversy over drones built under Jonathan, Buhari govts bySamuel Ogundipe. https://www.premiumtimesng.com/news/top-news/259041-nigerian-air-force-explains-controversy-drones-built-jonathan-buhari-govts.html?tztc=1

176 Prof. Yemi Osinbajo communicates President Buhari's take to the Nigeria military in the face of the menace posed by Boko Haram in Nigeria. Defend Nigeria with Your Lives, Osinbajo Tells Military. https://www.thisdaylive.com/index.php/2019/07/11/defend-nigeria-with-your-lives-osinbajo-tells-military/

177 Ibid

region of Cameroon[178]. In order to centralize the BIR's air surveillance, the Groupement d'Observation Aérienne (GOA) was formed[179].

In 2013, Boko Haram extended her activities into far north region of Cameroon from Nigeria[180]. With the emerging menace by Boko Haram, the government set up various military operations and deployed additional soldiers to fight Boko Haram in the north of the country. As the jihadi group was fighting on multiple fronts, that is Chad, Cameroon and Nigeria, the countries decided to come together an form a multinational joined task force to eradicate the menace posed by the group. Cameroon beganusing light Israeli Orbiter II drones (class I) in its operations[181] and it bought five additional light ScanEagle drones (class I) from the US[182]. The drones were used for surveillance and supported artillery strikes. The drones were based in Salak (Trafford & Turse, 2017), a Cameroonian base to which US military personnel had unrestricted access. Despite the appeal of some citizens in other countries on communication on counter terrorism, so far *Operation Alpha and Operation Thunder* are evidence of success of Cameroon's elite force.

Somalia

In 1991, a civilian war sparked after the fall of Somalian regime, benchmark human security challenges in the

---

178 The New Humanitarian. Rapid intervention military unit strays from its mission. https://www.thenewhumanitarian.org/report/80065/cameroon-rapid-intervention-military-unit-strays-its-mission

179 https://www.scramble.nl/planning/orbats/cameroon/cameroon-air-force

180 https://rieas.gr/researchareas/global-issues/afro-euro-affairs/4685-boko-haram-in-the-far-north-region-of-cameroon-what-next

181 Air Forces Monthly, April 2016, p.84.

182 AFCEA, 'Insitu to Provide Scan Eagle to Kenya and Cameroon', 30 September 2015. Accessed at: https://www.afcea.org/content/Blog-insitu-provide-scan-eagle-kenya-and-cameroon

country. In 2000, a Transitional National Government was established, which was followed by the Transitional Federal Government (TFG) in 2004 (Bradbury, 2010). Part of the country was controlled by Islamic Courts Union (ICU) and by 2006, the ICU was in charge of much of southern Somalia[183].

In 2007, the TFG, with support of the United States, Ethiopian troops and African Union peacekeepers, dismantled the ICU[184]. The ICU later separated into different factions, including al-Shabaab, which the U.S. categorizes as a terrorist organization. Since then, al-Shabaab has become a cancer in the horn of Africa[185].

A surveillance drone piloted by soldier of AUMISOM on April 29, 2014 over the town of Qoryooley, Somalia.

183 Bradbury, M. (2010)State-building, Counterterrorism, and Licensing Humanitarianism in Somalia. https://fic.tufts.edu/assets/state-building-somalia.pdf

184 Saving a Country without a State: Foreign Intervention and State Capacity in 21st Century Somalia by John Collison. https://polisci.ucsd.edu/undergrad/departmental-honors-and-pi-sigma-alpha/John-Collison_Senior-Honors_2019.pdf

185 Al Shabaab: The Cancer In East Africa by Saron Messembe Obia. https://iacspsea.org/v1/page.php?id=47

In 2011, Somalian President Sharif posed that, the U.S. drone strikes strengthen and weaken the government, as the drones helps fight against "criminals" but are also an infringement of the country's sovereignty (Kurpershoek, R. et al 2021). Although the American drones interfere with Somalia's sovereignty, Sharif equally authorized the U.S. to increase its assistance to the Somali military[186].

However, some Somali analysts like Abdillahi Sheikh Abukar, the Executive Director of the Somali Human Rights Association, an independent, non-governmental organization in Somalia, evoked the harm caused by drones on civilians and they denial of responsibility by foreign actors (Abukar, 2018). Others like Mahad Dhoore warned a Somalian member of parliament, al-Shabaab will use the foreign attacks in its recruitment drives and propaganda[187].

Non-state Actors

In Africa, violent non state actors are weaponizing *COTS drones*. Armed groups purchase these drones from hobbyists at a very cheap rate[188]. In West Africa, the *Islamic State West Africa Province* (ISWAP), commonly known as Boko Haram, is active in Nigeria, Chad, Niger and northern Cameroon purchased 1,500 to 3,500 fighters[189]. ISWAP has also

---

186   Ibid

187   Ibid

188   United Nations Security Council, 15 January 2019, 'Letter dated 15 January 2019 from the Chair of the Security Council Committee pursuant to resolutions 1267 (1999), 1989 (2011) and 2253 (2015) concerning Islamic State in Iraq and the Levant (Da'esh), Al-Qaida and associated individuals, groups, undertakings and entities addressed to the President of the Security Council', p. 23. Accessed at: https://www.un.org/sc/ctc/ wp-content/uploads/2019/02/N1846950_EN.pdf

189   United Nations Security Council, 15 January 2019, p. 12.

developed its own drones for reconnaissance, surveillance operations and which is a menace for West African states[190].

Since 2015, the *Islamic State in the Greater Sahel* (ISGS) has operated in the West African countries such as; Mali, Niger and Burkina Faso[191]. ISGS is also known to use COTS drones in Mali for surveillance purposes[192].

In North Africa, armed groups are operating drones too. The Egyptian General Commander of the Armed Forces revealed in 2018 that it captured a drone used by so-called "terrorists" in the Sinai region during a military operation[193]. Drones are equally use to monitor and control troops during operations. The Algerian Ministry of Defence published in the ministry's journal that it had captured 11 drones belonging to "terrorists" in Algeria in 2019[194]. It is possible that more non-state actors in Africa make use of COTS drones.

---

190   S. Crino & A. Dreby, Small Wars Journal, 'Drone Technology Proliferation in Small Wars', 10 February 2019. Accessed at: https:// smallwarsjournal. com/jrnl/art/drone-technology-proliferation-small-wars   United   Nations Security Council, 15 January 2019, p. 12. D. Searcey, 'Boko Haram is back. With better drones', The New York Times, 13 September 2019. Accessed at: https://www.nytimes.com/2019/09/13/world/africa/nigeria-boko-haram. html

191   United States Department of State Publication, 2019, 'Country Reports on Terrorism 2018', p. 293. Accessed at: https://www.justice.gov/eoir/page/ file/1215411/download

192   'Mali: à Indelimane, l'armée était en alerte', RFI, 5 November 2019. Accessed at: http://www.rfi.fr/fr/afrique/20191105-mali-indelimane-armee-etait-alerte International Centre for Counter-Terrorism – The Hague, 26 March 2020, [Video].

193   Egypt: A Repression Made in France. Exports of Weapons and Surveillance Technologies.   https://www.fidh.org/IMG/pdf/382873255-egypt-a-repression-made-in-france.pdf

194   Bilan des opérations 2018 : Résultats probants dans la lutte antiterroriste', In «El Djeich Num. 666», January 2019, pp. 20 – 21.

Case of Boko Haram in West Africa

Before Boko Haram was considered a local terrorist group, but today is has been given and international criminal tag. After changing its leadership structure in 2009, Boko Haram initiated a tactical adaptation process by copying the tactics of international extremist organizations. When Abubakar Shekau became Boko Haram's leader, he reconfigured the organization and tactics, while adopting the ideological perspective of the organization to a Salafi position (BALKAN, 2019). He also applied DAESH tactics by organizing assassinations, abducting people, selling women as slaves, and used them as suicide bombers.

Boko Haram committed a SVBIED attack against the United Nations building on August 26, 2011[195]. The group's use of women as suicide bombers and adoption of DAESH's acts of terror is evident that the group is ready to use drones as well. The first use of drones by Boko Haram was reported by the newspaper L'Oeil du Sahel on September 4, 2017. The news read 'Boko Haram utilizes drones in Cameroon and Nigeria for reconnaissance, surveillance, and attack'.

In a 16-minute propaganda video released by Boko Haram in January 2018 (Balkan, 2019)[196]the seventh minute shows the use of drones for reconnaissance /surveillance over the areas where security forces are deployed[197]. However, no drone strike has been carried out or claimed by the group.

---

195 Threat Tactics Report:Boko Haram by TRADOC G-2 ACEThreats Integration. https://info.publicintelligence.net/USArmy-BokoHaram.pdf

196 https://setav.org/en/assets/uploads/2019/12/R146En.pdf

197 Ibid

CHAPTER THREE

AIRSPACE CONTROL IN DEVELOPED COUNTRIES

Most African countries do not have law regulating the airspace and which adapt to contemporary security challenges. For example, the flying balloon over U.S. territory which was attributed to the Chinese spying on her counterpart. In appealing for African states to review or adopt law relating to modern warfare, some law in developed countries have been reviewed below.

United States of America

According to the *Federal Aviation Administration* (FAA), three government entities are responsible for operational control and security of the airspace adjacent to the contiguous United States: The Federal Aviation Administration (FAA), the *Department of Homeland Security* (DHS), and the *Department of Defense* (DoD)[198]. When Congress passed the *Aviation Drug Trafficking Control Act in 1984* and the *Federal Aviation Administration Drug Enforcement Assistance Act in 1988*, the FAA broadened (Hanchett,

---

198 Evaluation of the Multifunction Phased Array Radar Planning Process (2008). The National Academies Press. Washington, DC. https://nap. nationalacademies.org/read/12438/chapter/4

1991)[199] its mandate to include aerial drug trafficking. Congress enlisted the assistance of the FAA in combating aerial drug smuggling into the United States during the so-called 'War on Drugs' by granting them greater authority to enforce aircraft registration and certification of pilots.

Though empowered by Congress, the FAA's cardinal responsibility is aviation safety and not law enforcement. When it comes to law enforcement, including drug smuggling interdiction in border zones such as the U.S./Mexico border, the burden lies mainly on DHS. Within the Department of Homeland Security, the U.S. Coast Guard shares lead agency responsibility with U.S. Customs and Border Protection in drug interdiction, including aerial drug smuggling interdiction, although the Coast Guard's primary drug interdiction focus is in the maritime environment[200].

The 1989 Defense Authorization Bill assigned the DoD as the lead agency for detection and tracking of drug smuggling aircraft transiting through the airspace and maritime approaches into U.S. territorial borders. The FAA, DHS, and the DoD all play a role in some aspect of aerial drug trafficking interdiction (Schmersahl, 2018).

Early multinational agreements addressing the geopolitical intricacies of international air travel emerged from the ***Paris Convention of 1919***. One principle proposed and agreed upon during the Paris Convention was "the recognition that

---

199 Hanchett (1991) Role of the Federal Aviation Administration in the Control of Aviation Drug-Trafficking. Journal of Air Law and Commerce Volume: 56 Issue: 4 Dated: (Summer 1991) Pages: 999-1025. https://www.ojp.gov/ncjrs/virtual-library/abstracts/role-federal-aviation-administration-control-aviation-drug

200 Fifty Feet Above The Wall: Cartel Drones In The U.S.–Mexico Border Zone Airspace, And What To Do About Them by Aaron R. Schmersahl https://apps.dtic.mil/sti/pdfs/AD1052881.pdf

every State has complete and exclusive sovereignty over the airspace above its territory."

The 1944 Chicago Convention on International Civil Aviation expanded on the Paris agreement. Then Chicago Convention established the ***International Civil Aviation Organization*** (ICAO), an agency that became part of the United Nations. ICAO's purpose is to develop the internationally accepted rules for airspace, and to define the rights of signatories which include the United States and Mexico. Article 1 of the 1944 Chicago Convention reaffirms the state's exclusive sovereignty of the airspace over its territory.

U.S. law clearly defines who has sovereignty in the airspace. Title 49 of U.S. code 40103 states that the federal government has exclusive sovereignty in U.S. airspace. The federal government asserted control over airspace early on in response to aviation industry leaders requests for federal action to establish standards for aviation safety. Early aviation industry leaders believed that without government regulation the aviation industry could not reach its full commercial potential. After some urging, Congress passed the ***Air Commerce Act*** in 1926. This legislation assigned exclusive sovereignty of U.S. airspace to the federal government. From then on airspace control took on a new shape with the issuing of air traffic rules, pilot licensing requirements, aircraft certifications, and charting of airways across U.S. territory.

The commercial drones the cartels are using typically fly in what the ***International Civil Aviation Organization*** (ICAO) classifies as Class G airspace. Class G airspace exits below 1200 feet ***Above Ground Level*** (AGL), or in some areas below 700 feet when near an airfield. Class G airspace is 'uncontrolled' by ***Air Traffic Control*** (ATC), meaning you can fly an aircraft in the airspace without coordinating with air traffic controllers.

Similar to U.S. drone regulations, drones in Mexico may not be operated in areas that are designated as prohibited or restricted and can only be flown during the daytime hours. Drones cannot drop objects or material that could cause injury to people or damage to property. Any drone operator that wants to fly outside the requirements and limitations described above must request approval from Mexico's aeronautical authority.

The United States and Mexico both adhere to ICAO standards, both countries currently limit drone flights to Class G airspace, unless waived by proper authority. According to the FAA, commercial drone flights are restricted to altitudes below 400 feet AGL, day-time flight only, and the pilot must maintain **visual line of sight** (VLOS) with the drone at all times. Mexico adopted similar measures, specifically the restrictions of daytime flight only, and the requirement for pilots to maintain visual sight with their drone in flight while adhering to visual flight rules.

The restriction that pilots maintain visual line of sight with their drone and fly during daytime only is an effective way to control drones on the border. If a drone is flying at night in the border zone, which the narco-drones highlighted in chapter 2 were, then drones detected flying at night in the border zone can be assumed to be hostile or possibly engaged in illicit activities.

The FAA argues that "it has authority to regulate aircraft in U.S. airspace," and drones are, by definition aircraft, albeit unmanned. Title 49 of U.S. Code section 40102(a)(6) defines "aircraft" as "any contrivance invented, used, or designed to navigate or fly in the air." FAA regulation 14 CFR section 1.1 defines an aircraft simply as "a device that is used or intended to be used for flight in the air." Title 49 U.S. Code section 40103 stipulates the administrator of the FAA "shall develop plans and policy for the use of navigable airspace and assign by regulation or order the use of the airspace necessary to ensure the safety of aircraft and the efficient use of airspace." Although plans for integrating drones into the airspace are trickling out of the FAA, the FAA is often criticized for being too slow when implementing rules and regulations.

The FAA has provided a framework for incorporating drones into the National Airspace System due to industry pressures in areas like land surveillance, disaster response, wildlife tracking, search and rescue, photography, and law enforcement. Similar to manned aircraft, the FAA regulates drones by requiring mandatory registration of aircraft and pilot certifications.

The number of people purchasing drones for work or recreation is rising, and the trend of drones entering the airspace does not seem to be slowing down. Over 770,000 drone operators have registered their drones ever since the FAA began requiring registration in 2015. That is over double the number of manned aircraft registrations in the U.S. and the gap continues to grow (Schmersahl,2018).

The statutory authority of the FAA to regulate drones in the airspace has its limits, and those limits are codified in law, namely the FAA Modernization and Reform Act. A U.S. Court of Appeals for the District of Columbia recently ruled that the FAA's registration requirement for small drones, which until included drones operated as "model aircraft," directly violates the FAA's statutory authority. The FAA Modernization and Reform Act states the FAA "may not promulgate any rule or regulation regarding a model aircraft."

Congress has directed the FAA to "promote safe flight of civil aircraft" and to standardize the operation of aircraft in the United States, as directed by 49 U.S.C. § 44701(a). In response, the FAA has taken on a regulatory role, requiring drone operators to register their drones, take a knowledge exam, and be vetted by the *Transportation Security Administration* (TSA). The FAA's attempt to control drone use in the U.S. by implementing a drone registration requirement for all drones seems like a good approach for getting accountability for drone pilots that may perpetrate airspace violations. However, drone owners who say that they fly drones for recreation or as a hobby took issue with the registration requirement.

In March of 2017, hobbyist drone owner *John Taylor* filed a lawsuit challenging the FAA's authority to require registration of all categories of drones[201]. After examination, the U.S. Court of Appeals for the District of Columbia invalidated the registration requirement for drones considered 'model aircraft' because the court found the registration requirement conflicted with guidance set forth in the Congressional *FAA Modernization and Reform Act*. The Act states drones "capable of sustained flight in the atmosphere, flown within visual line-of-sight of the person operating it, and flown for hobby or recreational purposes in the category of 'model aircraft." (Schmersahl, 2018) If a drone is purchased in the US, and weighs less than 55 pounds—which by all accounts the narco-drones and respective payloads found to be used by the drug cartels have all weighed less than 55 pounds— then the operator does not need to register the drone with the FAA as it would meet the requirements to be considered a model aircraft.

The *Federal Aviation Administration Modernization and Reform Act of 2012* is a starting point for understanding the

---

201 https://www.geekwire.com/2017/hobbyist-faa-drone-registration/ https:// jrupprechtlaw.com/drone-registration-lawsuit/

trajectory of federal airspace regulation for drone operations in the United States. Transnational criminal organizations operating on the Mexico side of the border have no impetus for adhering to U.S. federal regulation, which begs the question what is needed to protect against drones coming from Mexico.

Japan

With the proliferation of new technologies and the quest for global dominance, Japan has not develop principles regulating her airspace but also enforce her development of technological tools to face the new world order. The following laws and regulations governing the flights of unmanned aircraft vehicles (drones) ("UAVs") in Japan:

(a) Civil Aeronautics Act (the "CAA");

(b) Act Prohibiting UAVs' Flights Over Important Facilities and Surrounding Areas (the "Drone Act");

(c) Civil Code;

(d) Radio Wave Act; and

(e) Local Regulations (jyourei) legislated by local governments[202].

The CAA is the main legislation for aviation safety in Japan, and the **Ministry of Land, Infrastructure, Transport and Tourism** (the "MLIT") is the one in charge of regulating the aviation sector. However, CAA was amended to include safety rules based on the emergence of unmanned aircraft vehicles, and after a drone was found on the roof of the Prime Minister's office on April 22, 2015[203]. It's worth noting

---

202 https://iclg.com/practice-areas/aviation-laws-and-regulations/5-regulations-on-drone-flights-in-japan/

203 https://iclg.com/practice-areas/aviation-laws-and-regulations/5-regulations-on-drone-flights-in-japan

that, the law was amended in less than eight months by the Japanese parliament.

The Drone Act

This law was enacted on March 17, 2016 and took effect on April 7, 2016, just before the G7 Foreign Ministers' Meeting in Hiroshima, Japan. It prohibits flights of UAVs over important facilities, including the Houses of Parliament, the Prime Minister's Official Residence, buildings of the government Ministries, the Supreme Court, the Imperial Palace, and nuclear plants, and areas within approximately 300 metres of these facilities. The purpose of the law is to prevent danger in the facilities and to secure the central affairs of the State, maintenance of good international relationships and public safety. Thus, it differs from the purpose of the CAA, which is to secure the safety of aviation. The Drone Act was amended in 2019 and 2020 to prohibit the operation of UAVs over important facilities designated by the Ministry of Defense and over major airports.

The definition of UAVs under the Drone Act is basically the same as under the CAA. However, this law prohibits the flights of UAVs weighing less than 200 grams[204]. Under this law, UAV flights over important facilities and surrounding areas are allowed only if the operator

(a) Is an administrator of the facilities or has obtained the consent of the facility administrator,

(b) Owns the land or has obtained the consent of the owner of the land, or

(c) Flies the UAV to perform services for the State or local governments, and submits a notification to the

---

204 https://iclg.com/practice-areas/aviation-laws-and-regulations/5-regulations-on-drone-flights-in-japan

Public Safety Commission through the Police Station with jurisdiction over the facilities, 48 hours prior to the flight. Any person who violates the Drone Act may be subject to imprisonment for up to one year or a fine of up to JPY 500,000.

Radio Wave Act

Japan is one of the countries in the world with good drone regulation. The Radio Wave Act provided adequate definition on operators of drones and its link to telecommunication. Radio Station (*musenkyoku*) refers to an electric facility which transmits and receives radio frequencies and its operator. More so, the law provides that the operator of a Radio Station must have the qualifications designated under the Radio Wave Act and its ordinance. Japan equally has regulations on system which deals with trial license to use a device on UAVs as well as mobile phone. However, the trial license provides that, UAVs may transmit large volumes of data without passing through a controller, while flying over large areas covered by multiple base stations[205].

In 2020, the Japanese Ministry of Internal Affairs and Communications, whose the main regulator of the *Radio Wave Act*, define technical requirements for providing full, non-trial licenses for any device-equipped UAVs[206].

Mexico

Mexico's Constitution of 1917 has specific provisions as to the use of UAV. As a treatise has summarized: "The Mexican Constitution provides the legal basis for civil aviation."[207]

---

205 Ibid

206 https://iclg.com/practice-areas/aviation-laws-and-regulations/5-regula-tions-on-drone-flights-in-japan

207 Rosa Ma. Ramírez de Arellano,MEXICO Space Regulations. ICAO / UNOOSA Symposium15–17 March 2016, Abu Dhabi, United Arab

Regarding securing drones bases and restricting the operation of drone by non-Mexican operators, article 27 of Mexico's Constitution equally forbids foreign ownership of land within the restricted zone comprising of 100 kilometers from the border or 50 kilometers from the coastline[208].

The April 2015 Mexican Drone Regulations Signed by Gilberto Lopez Meyer, minister of the ***Director General de Aeronáutica Civil*** (DGAC), the new Mexican Drone Regulations (***Circular Obligatoria CO AV-23/10 R2***) pertaining to drone usage in Mexican airspace was endorsed on April 8, 2015[209]. The DGAC issued another communication in April of 2015 to highlight and explain the mandatory Mexican Drone Regulations or Circular ***Obligatoria***, the DGAC had just adopted.

According to SOLTERO (2016) , based on Mexican Drone Regulations, drones are "RPAS" or Remotely Piloted Aircraft Systems[210]. The expressed purposes for these new regulations were to maintain public safety and the safety of operators due to the increased usage of RPAS/drones in Mexico. The April 2015 DGAC Regulations supplant the regulations previously in effect since issued in 2010. The DCGA made compliance with the Mexican Drone Regulations mandatory for all RPAS/drone operators.

Emirates. https://www.icao.int/Meetings/SPACE2016/Presentations/6%20-%20R.%20Arellano%20-%20Mexican%20Space%20Agency.pdf

208 James J. Kelly,Article 27 and Mexican Land Reform: The Legacy of Zapata's Dream, 25 Colum. Hum. Rts. L. Rev. 541 (1993-1994).Available at:https://scholarship.law.nd.edu/law_faculty_scholarship/668

209https://www.mcginnislaw.com/assets/htmldocuments/Introduction_to_Mexican_Drone_Regulations__Exhibit.pdf

210 SOLTERO (2016) An Introduction to Mexican Drone Regulations. https://www.mcginnislaw.com/assets/htmldocuments/Introduction_to_Mexican_Drone_Regulations__Exhibit.pdf

A. The Mexican Drone Regulations classify the RPAS/drones by three categories based on weight in Section 7.1 and has a table in the regulation itself:

1. Micro (Up to 2 kg) which do not require DGAC authorization.

2. Light (Between 2 and 25 kg) where if for commercial use, DGAC authorization is required14; but if for recreational use only they may only be used within authorized *aeromodelismo* clubs and the requirements and subject to the limitations applicable to those clubs. There are also speed limits of 161 km/hour and a minimum height of 152 meters (500 feet).

3. Heavy (Greater than 25kg) Detailed DGAC regulations and restrictions apply and the operator must have a pilot license.

B. Flight/operational restrictions applicable to all RPAS/drones:

The following is a summary and translated list of Section 7.2 I prepared, which sets forth a list of requirements and limitations that apply to all RPAS/drone operations:

a) No operator may allow the falling or throwing (even with a parachute) of any object or material from a RPAS/drone that could cause damage or harm (*daño*) to any person or property.

b) No operation may occur if the operator cannot do so safely as determined by a pre-flight inspection.

c) At all times operations must be in class G airspace except with a strict and prior coordination with the *Servicios de Tránsitos Aéreo*/air traffic control.

d) No operations/flights allowed in areas designated as prohibited, restricted, or hazardous.

e) No transporting of dangerous materials or substances prohibited by law nor to use or transport arms or explosives.

f) The operator must maintain control of the flight path/trajectory of flight at all times.

g) The operator is responsible for its operation, and in the event of an accident, of any damages or harms (***daños***) caused by the RPAS/drone.

h) The operator is responsible for the misuse of any information obtained during the operation of the RPAS/drone.

i) The operator must comply with all laws, regulations, and norms, whether federal or local, related to national security, public safety, and the protection of privacy, intellectual property among others.

j) The person responsible for the RPAS/drone may not operate the RPAS/drone in a manner that is negligent or that endangers a third person's life or property.

k) Operations may only occur during daylight hours absent specially obtained authorization from the aerospace authority for nighttime flights or IFR.

l) The operator must yield the right of way to any aircraft ***tripulada*** unless the RPAS/drone and the other aircraft are under positive control of the ***Servicios de Tránsitos Aéreo/air traffic control***.

m) RPAS/drones may not be operated from moving vehicles unless they are on water and that it is necessary for adequate or proper operation.

n) Foreign registered RPAS/drones or RPAS/drones operated by foreigners with scientific objectives must apply for a permit from the ***Secretaría de la Defensa Nacional*** in accordance with other federal laws.

There exist certain restrictions in the Mexican Drone Regulations which limits operations/flights as follows:

➢ 9.2 km (5 nautical miles) from any controlled airports absent prior coordination with the Servicios de Tránsitos Aéreo/air traffic control;

➢ 3.7 km (2 nautical miles) from any uncontrolled aeródromos; or

➢ 900 meters(0.5 nautical miles) from any heliport.

For Micro RPAS/drones, additional requirements and limitations are located in Section 8 of the Mexican Drone Regulations. These include that the maximum height of operations is 122 meters (400 feet) above the ground, the minimum height of operations is 46 meters (150 feet) above the ground, and the RPAS/drone must be operated within the light of sight and within a horizontal distance of 447 meters or 1,500 feet from the operator according to Section 8.1.1. a) and b). There are also speed restrictions applicable to takeoff and operational speed depending on the weight of the RPAS/drone.

The Mexican Drone Regulations require micro RPAS/drones to be made of destructible material and designed to minimise risk to any person or object that collides with the unit (SOLTERO, 2016). If used for commercial purposes, then the operator must have an applicable insurance policy covering harm (daños) to third persons.

Additional DGAC regulations for commercial use of heavy RPAS/drones in excess of 25 kg as provided for in Section

10. The recreational use of heavy RPAS/drones are subject to the same regulations applicable to the recreational use of light drones. For commercial uses of heavy RPAS/drones, the DGAC regulations have other requirements including requiring the operator to be a licensed pilot as set forth in Appendix C of the Mexican Drone Regulations. For the commercial use of heavy RPAS/drones in Mexico, there is a detailed permitting process which provides for testing procedures specified in Section 10.2 and its subparts. Section 10.2.3 contains prerequisites to obtaining a permit which include personal information as well as proof of an applicable insurance policy covering harm (daños) to third persons. RPAS/drones registered under this regulation are required to have a certificate of enrollment and must have the flag of their nationality and registration information painted on the RPAS/drones themselves for identification purposes.

A manual of operations with prescribed procedures is also a requirement. While the DGAC has issued the Mexican Drone Regulations, some Mexican drone operators seek greater clarity and guidance. In a December 14, 2015 article, Edwin Gomez Torres, identified as president of the Mexican Drones Association is quoted as noting that the Mexican Drone Regulations "are quite basic" and lacking additional information (SOLTERO, 2016). He equally out pinmed that, Mexican Drone Regulations "do not include penalties or list responsibilities.

CHAPTER FOUR

DRONE OPERATIONS IN THE GLOBALIZATION ERA

The Charter of the United Nations (UN Charter) of June 1945 is the most important legal document in international law in relation to drone operations in the 21ˢᵗ century. Of central importance to what is often referred to as the Constitution of the United Nations which focuses on the Use of Force (or Prohibition of Force), codified in Article 2 (4) of the UN Charter. With the emergence of insecurity, international law (*ius cogens*)[211] and customary international law[212] endorse the use of force in situations where national and international security are threatened.

Use of Force And The Principle of Sovereignty

Article 2 (4) Use of Force

All Members shall refrain in their international relations from the threat or use of force against the territorial integrity

---

211 International Court of Justice (ICJ), 'Military and Paramilitary Activities in and against Nicaragua (Nicaragua v. United States of America)', Merits, judgment of 27 JUN 1986, ICJ Reports 1986, 94, clause 190-1, http://www.icj-cij.org/docket/files/70/6503.pdf; Yoram Dinstein, War, Aggression and Self-Defence, (Cambridge: Cambridge University Press, 2011), p. 87.

212 International Court of Justice (ICJ): 'Military and Paramilitary Activities in and against Nicaragua (Nicaragua v. United States of America)', Merits, judgment of 27 JUN 1986, ICJ Reports 1986, 94, clause 188-9, http://www.icj-cij.org/docket/files/70/6503.pdf.

or political independence of any state, or in any other manner inconsistent with the Purposes of the United Nations[213].

In case a state uses an armed drone in combat operations inside the territory of another state, this constitutes the use of military force and could equally be a violation of Article 2 (4) UN Charter[214]. This stance appeals to state practice concerning the use of military force. Thus, the Use of Force article is supposed to be interpreted broadly, every use of military force inside another state's territory is to be regarded as a violation of Article 2 (4). Therefore, a drone entering another state's airspace and launching an air to ground missile to kill, in a targeted manner, persons on the ground (among them, conceivably, uninvolved civilians) constitutes a possible violation of Article 2 (4), UN Charter[215].

A drone attack that is a violation of the Use of Force also violates the Principle of Sovereignty and the Prohibition of Intervention[216]. The UN member states enjoy the same rights and privileges (irrespective of size and influence), and individual states must not indiscriminately interfere in the internal affairs of another state.41 The Principle of

---

213 United Nations Charter, Chapter I: Purposes and Principles. https://www. un.org/en/about-us/un-charter/chapter-1

214 Reisner, M. Current drone warfare in the light of the prohibition of interventions: The use of drones in armed conflicts in Afghanistan, Iraq, Israel, Yemen, Libya, Mali, Pakistan, the Philippines, Somalia, and Syria. https://viennalawreview.com/index.php/vlr/article/view/52/25/

215 When drafting the UN Charter, the intention of the UN was to prevent any acts of aggression or other breaches of the peace. This includes any use of military force; cf.: Dieter Dörr and Peter Reifenberg, Gezielte Tötung erlaubt? Der Fall Osama bin Laden, (Mainz: Bischöfliches Ordinariat Mainz, 2011), p. 9-10.

216 Reisner, M. Current drone warfare in the light of the prohibition of interventions: The use of drones in armed conflicts in Afghanistan, Iraq, Israel, Yemen, Libya, Mali, Pakistan, the Philippines, Somalia, and Syria. https://viennalawreview.com/index.php/vlr/article/view/52/25/

Sovereignty is derived from Article 2 (1) of the UN Charter and is recognized in customary international law. It states:

Article 2 (1) Principle of Sovereignty

The Organization is based on the principle of the sovereign equality of all its members[217].

Using an armed drone inside another state's territory may thus be a violation of the Principle of Sovereignty[218].

Exceptions to the UN Charter's Use of Force

The use of armed drones on another nations territory can also be justified, based on two exceptions to the UN Charter's Use of Force, of which the first is Article 51. It affirms the Right to Self-Defense for a state or a subject of international law which means that states may defend themselves in the event of an armed attack.

Article 51: Right to Self-Defense

Nothing in the present Charter shall impair the inherent right of individual or collective self-defence if an armed attack occurs against a Member of the United Nations, until the Security Council has taken the measures necessary to maintain international peace and security[219]. Measures taken by Members in the exercise of this right of self-defence shall be immediately reported to the Security Council and shall

---

217 Art 2 of the UN Charter.– also cf. Art. 2 (7) of the UN Charter, 'Nothing contained in the present Charter shall authorize the United Nations to intervene in matters which are essentially within the domestic jurisdiction of any state […]' This is connected to the Principle of Sovereignty, Art. 2 (1) of the UN Charter.

218 Bernhard Kempen and Christian Hillgruber, Völkerrecht, 2nd edn, (Munich: C.H.Beck, 2012), p. 167-8.

219 United Nations Charter, Chapter VII: Action with Respect to Threats to the Peace, Breaches of the Peace, and Acts of Aggression. https://www.un.org/en/about-us/un-charter/chapter-7

not in any way affect the authority and responsibility of the Security Council under the present Charter to take at any time such action as it deems necessary in order to maintain or restore international peace and security[220].

The second exception to the Use of Force is a Security Council Resolution concerning military sanctions pursuant to Chapter VII. Since the creation of the UN Charter, specifically Article 2, any war (or armed conflict according to the definition set out in the Geneva Conventions between states, by definition), violates international law. The right to wage war (ius ad bellum) only applies in exceptional cases, all set out in the UN Charter.

In 1974, **UN General Assembly Resolution 3314** defined pertinent terms in further detail. It is, for the most part, an interpretation of Article 39 of the UN Charter. A war of aggression is thus a crime against peace, and the state responsible can be held to account according to international law. Furthermore, direct as well as indirect force, and the threat of force, are illegal. Even the subjects of international law may use military force only pursuant to Chapter VII or Article 39, UN Charter, respectively[221].

If the peace is threatened or breached, or acts of aggression are carried out, the United Nations can take measures – even without the affected state's agreement – to restore international peace. To this end, a suitable mandate is granted. Article 39 UN Charter defines the issue, while Article 41 (measures not involving the use of armed force) and Article 42 (military measures) set out the benchmarks of possible approaches[222].

---

220 Ibid

221 Art. 39 of the UN Charter.

222 Art. 39, Art. 40, Art. 41 of the UN Charter.

Apart from measures of self-defense pursuant to Article 51 or the authorization of military force pursuant to Chapter VII, the following can also be the case: (1) a state expressly requests an intervention inside its territory to be carried out by another state, (2) a state requests the support of another state with counterinsurgency measures to be carried out on its territory, and (3) a state requests the support of another state in carrying out domestic police tasks on its territory[223].

Article 2 and Article 51 of the UN Charter are therefore highly relevant as regards the use of drones. A closer look shows that it is, above all, the exceptions to the Use of Force which are highly important for an assessment of current warfare by means of unmanned reconnaissance and weapon systems; especially if subjects of international law use such weapons as means of warfare above the territory of other states[224]. However, the essential point is that it is not the use of armed or unarmed drone systems that is relevant, but the manner in which these are used by states vis-à- vis other states or above their territory[225]. In this, an unmanned drone differs in no way from a manned bomber or reconnaissance aircraft.

---

223   Chatham House (ed.), 'International Law and the Use of Drones. Summary of the International Law Discussion Group meeting held at Chatham House on 21 October 2010', http://www.chathamhouse.org/sites/files/chathamhouse/field/field_document/il211010drones.pdf.

224   Robert Frau, 'Unbemannte Luftfahrzeuge im international bewaffneten Konflikt', (2011) 24 Institutfür Friedenssicherungsrecht und Humanitäres Völkerrecht: Humanitäres Völkerrecht -Informationsschriften, Journal of International Law of Peace and Armed Conflict, special edition 'Nicht-bemannte Waffensysteme und Humanitäres Völkerrecht', no. 2, p. 60-1.

225   Chatham House, 'International Law and the Use of Drones. Summary of the International Law Discussion Group meeting held at Chatham House on 21 October 2010', p. 2.

Current arguments and justifications of drone operations

The US government argues that its current global war against terrorists (relying to a high extent on the deployment of armed drones) is legally justified pursuant to Article 51 UN Charter, i.e. the right to self-defence. All state and non-state actors with hostile intentions towards the USA are legitimate targets. International law experts argue that, applying Article 51 to Afghanistan was and is legal.

The *UN Security Council passed Resolutions 1368 and 1373*, which gave the USA the legitimization to defend itself against a non-state actor, in this case Al Qaeda[226]. This made operations in Afghanistan from 2001 to 2002 legitimate, for the government requested support. What is the case, however, with the attacks carried out in Iraq, Pakistan, Yemen, Syria, or Somalia? Also Iraq, or rather its legitimate government, elected after the fall of Saddam Hussein, asked the USA for support in its fight against insurgent groups and ISIS. As was the case with Afghanistan's request for help, the Prohibition of Force did not apply here[227].

It can be assumed that in the case of Pakistan the attacks have been carried out (at least sometimes) with the approval of the local government. There is a reasonable certainty that the Pakistani government took a duplicitous approach vis-à-vis its population, denouncing US drone attacks publicly while tolerating them unofficially. How else could there be credible reports that there were, or still are, US drone bases on Pakistani territory? From 2001 to 2011, for example, US MQ-1 Predator drones were repeatedly spotted at Shamsi

226   Chatham House, 'International Law and the Use of Drones. Summary of the International Law Discussion Group meeting held at Chatham House on 21 October 2010', p. 5.

227   Chatham House, 'International Law and the Use of Drones. Summary of the International Law Discussion Group meeting held at Chatham House on 21 October 2010', p. 5.

airport, in Beluchistan, 200 km[228] to the south of Quetta (seat of the Taliban's so-called Quetta Shura). They were allegedly operated by the CIA and the US Air Force. Only after an incident in which 24 Pakistani soldiers were killed by US combat aircraft in the border region between Afghanistan and Pakistan did Pakistan ban the USA from using the base, whereupon the USA vacated the site. If the USA really have pulled out of Pakistan, and if there really is no agreement between Pakistan and the USA regarding drone strikes on Pakistani territory, any attack would contravene the Prohibition of Force set out in the UN Charter and, therefore, also violate international law. In a similar case - Congo vs Uganda - the ***International Court of Justice*** (ICJ) found as follows: the fact that the Congolese military was unable to put an end to attacks on Uganda emanating from Congolese territory does not give Uganda the right to advance its own forces into Congolese territory[229].

Another case is that of Yemen. Which the nation request for assistance from the US to help fight against Al Qaeda. No U.S. base have been revealed in Yemen, though her neighbour Saudi Arabia harbours one. The advantage of a US drone base near the Yemeni border lies in the substantially reduced flight distance, which is, of course, shorter from Saudi Arabia than from Djibouti in Africa[230]. This results in a much higher loiter time of the UAVs or UCAVs above their targets.

---

228 Reisner, Current drone warfare in the light of the prohibition of interventions ; The use of drones in armed conflicts in Afghanistan, Iraq, Israel,Yemen, Libya, Mali, Pakistan, the Philippines, Somalia, and Syria. University of Vienna Law Review, Vol. 2:1 (2018), pp. 69-94. https://doi.org/10.25365/vlr-2018-2-1-69.

229 Armed Activities on the Territory of the Congo (Democratic Republic of the Congo v. Uganda). https://www.icj-cij.org/case/116

230 https://viennalawreview.com/index.php/vlr/article/view/52/25

The distance to the targets is one of the biggest challenges, according to the ISR Taskforce, Requirements and Analysis Division in its report ISR Support to Small Footprint CT Operations - Somalia/Yemen. A base's proximity to the targets to be reconnoitred makes a much longer observation period possible.

Somalia, which can be classified as a failed state, rule of law or governmental authority is doubtful. What, if any, recognized and legitimate national authority is there to request an intervention from a third party? The situation in Iraq and Syria is also problematic. In these cases, there is also no mandate for military operations against ISIS. As far as Iraq is concerned, at least the Iraqi government requested the support already mentioned. However, in Syria, some states (inter alia France) strikes with their manned and unmanned weapon systems invoke Article 51 of the UN Charter. It is still contested if the terror attacks in Paris really were an armed attack of high intensity (along the lines of 9/11), and if states can invoke Article 51 in dealing with terrorist organizations (and therefore non-states) such as ISIS.

As a result, the USA, but also Great Britain and France are acting in their attacks in Pakistan, Yemen, Syria, Somalia or broader Africa without a clear mandate under international law. On the other side, Russia might argue it is acting on the request of the Syrian state, but it is clearly violating international law in Ukraine. All of the them do not strike against clearly defined, enemy armed forces, but direct their attacks, on the basis of reconnaissance data they have generated, against groups and individuals, subsumed under the vague and politically highly problematic term terrorists. The examples cited reveal a grey area in international law that the USA and other actors occupy nolens volens. It's clear that these actors attempt, as part of warfare by means of drones, to interpret Article 2 (1) and (4) (Principle of

Sovereignty, Use of Force), as well as Article 51 (Right to Self-Defence) of the UN Charter to their own ends. The fact that drones are unmanned means that their loss produces little cause for concern. The USA is fully aware of this grey area. The government, therefore, attempts to depict its approach coherently vis-à-vis public interventions. The Obama Administration, for example, argued that, as opposed to the **Global War on Terror Doctrine** of the Bush years, it was engaged in an Armed Conflict against Al-Qaida, the Taliban and associated Forces[231].

The application of international humanitarian law based on the use of drones

In the event of an armed conflict, it must be the highest priority of the participating parties to limit or to contain its effects as much as possible. The fragmentation of states, the emergence of terrorism, totalitarianism, does not limit the application of international humanitarian law applies (ius in bello, law of armed conflict)[232] during internal wrangling or armed conflict. Relevant criteria are to be found in The Hague Conventions and the Geneva Conventions. International humanitarian law is applicable to two types of armed conflicts:

1. International armed conflicts

2. non-international armed conflicts[233]

This distinction is relevant insofar as fundamentally different conventions can be applied in the two situations. The

---

231 Roland Otto, Targeted Killings and International Law: With Special Regard to Human Rights and

International Humanitarian Law, (Heidelberg: Springer, 2012), pp. 22-4.

232 Knut Ipsen, Völkerrecht, 6th edn, (Munich: C.H.Beck, 2014), pp. 1175-6.

233 Dieter Fleck, The Handbook of International Humanitarian Law, 3rd edn, (New York: Oxford University Press, 2013), pp. 43-4.

following apply in international armed conflicts: *The Hague Conventions of 1899/1907, the four Geneva Conventions of 1949* (with the exception of Common Article 3), and *Protocol I of 1977* (relating to the Protection of Victims of International Armed Conflicts). Article 3 of the *Geneva Conventions of 1949* and *Protocol II of 1977* focuses on non-international conflicts.

Dieter Fleck, a well-recognized expert of international humanitarian law, states in his Handbook of International Humanitarian Law concerning the application of the different conventions in international armed conflicts:

An international armed conflict exists if one state uses force of arms against another state. This shall also apply to all cases of total or partial military occupation, even if this occupation meets with no armed resistance (Article 2, para. 2 common to the Geneva Conventions). The use of military force by individual persons or groups of persons will not suffice. It is irrelevant whether the parties to the conflict consider themselves to be at war with each other and how they describe this conflict[234].

Further on, he refers to the application of the different conventions in non-international armed conflicts: in a non-international armed conflict each party shall be bound to apply, as a minimum, fundamental humanitarian provisions of international law[235]. Regular armed forces should comply with the rules of international humanitarian law in the conduct of military operations in all armed conflicts however, such conflicts are characterized.

---

234 Cristopher Greenwood, 'Scope of Application of Humanitarian Law', in The Handbook of International Humanitarian Law, 2nd edn, Dieter Fleck (ed.), (New York: Oxford University Press, 2010), p. 46.

235 https://ihl-databases.icrc.org/en/ihl-treaties/gciii-1949/article-3

A number of states jointly intervening in a non-international armed conflict does not set a precedent for a change of the classification of the conflict. An armed conflict that is conducted solely on the territory of one state can, however, be regarded as an international armed conflict if a foreign state uses its armed forces to fight alongside insurgents against regular government forces. This situation immediately brings to mind the precarious legal situation in Ukraine. In the so-called ***Tadić case***[236], the ***International Criminal Tribunal for the former Yugoslavia (ICTY)*** stated that a non-international armed conflict applies

> [...] whenever there is protracted armed violence between governmental authorities

> and organized armed groups or between such groups within a State[237]

Experts in international law are debating whether a state's military intervention in another state's non-international armed conflict effects an internationalization of the whole conflict, or only between the two states involved. Thus, two types of conflict could take place concurrently. Common Article 3 defines a lower threshold for a non-international armed conflict than does Protocol II. This is why the terms non international armed conflict of low intensity (Common Article 3) and high intensity (Common Article 3 and Protocol II) are used[238]. Fleck concluded that;

---

236 International Humanitarian Law and the Tadic Case by Christopher Greenwood. http://www.ejil.org/pdfs/7/2/1365.pdf

237 International Criminal Tribunal for the former Yugoslavia (ICTY), 'The Prosecutor v. Dusko Tadic, Decision on the Defence Motion for Interlocutory Appeal on Jurisdiction', IT-94-1-A, 2 October 1995, para. 70.

238 Lars Schmidt, 'Das humanitäre Völkerrecht in modernen asymmetrischen Konflikten', Schriften zum Völkerrecht, vol. 198, (Berlin: Duncker & Humblot, 2012), pp. 23-5. - Gary D. Solis, The Law of Armed Conflict:

there is an important trend in the law towards expanding the scope of application of rules related to the conduct of hostilities originally contained only in the law of international armed conflict to situations of non-international armed conflict, while, at the same time, respecting the distinction which continues to exist in these two types of conflict on matters of status of the fighters.[239]

Protocol II presupposes a high level of organization among the insurgents, and, in addition, comprehensive, continuous, and coordinated fighting. Furthermore, the non-state conflict party must also be in control of a part of the state's territory. Whether this is the case will be difficult to tell, since the states involved will most probably deny that the non-state parties to the conflict are, in effect, already exercising this control. An example of such conflict is Ukraine. This particular situation is not even taken into account by Protocol II. Targeted killings are legal in an international armed conflict as long as they produce a real military advantage.

However, individuals who enjoy protected status or that of hors de combat must not be attacked. The fact that a target individual cannot be taken prisoner does not automatically justify a targeted killing. This especially applies to persons whose legal status as regards international legal norms cannot be exactly determined. Sanctioning anticipatory calculations in attacks ("There will be no survivors") is not legal (*No Survivor Policy or carrying out Follow-On Strikes*)[240].

International Humanitarian Law in War, (New York: Cambridge University Press, 2010), pp. 45-7.

239 Reisner, Current drone warfare in the light of the prohibition of interventions : The use of drones in armed conflicts in Afghanistan, Iraq, Israel,Yemen, Libya, Mali, Pakistan, the Philippines, Somalia, and Syria. University of Vienna Law Review, Vol. 2:1 (2018), pp. 69-94. https://doi.org/10.25365/vlr-2018-2-1-69.

240 Reisner, Current drone warfare in the light of the prohibition of interventions : The use of drones in armed conflicts in Afghanistan, Iraq, Israel,Yemen,

The result of such attack must be proportionate (Proportionality Assessment) as regards potential civilian casualties (Collateral Damage). It also applies to so-called bystanders, persons who are in the immediate vicinity of a possible drone strike's target individual. With civilians, another crucial question is to what extent their activities contribute to a participation in hostilities, depriving them from their protected status. International humanitarian law is a highly complex composite of interdependent norms which make it necessary for every situation to be assessed individually, without, however, losing sight of the whole. This similarly applies to non-international armed conflicts.

Drone strikes only comply with international humanitarian law if certain principles are fulfilled. The principle of distinction requires that only lawful targets (that means combatants or civilians directly participating in hostilities and military objective) are targeted intentionally. The principle of proportionality requires that the expected collateral damage is not excessive in relation to the anticipated military advantage. The principle of humanity requires the use of weapons that will not inflict unnecessary suffering.

Drone Strikes and State Responsibility: UN Perspective

The Use of Force and Consent from the Host State

Among other justifications, foreign powers have consistently invoked the consent given by African host states to attest to the lawfulness of drone strikes against suspected terrorists residing in their territory. France considers itself a party to the armed conflict in Mali at the invitation of the Malian government and relied on the consent of neighbouring countries to expand its counterterrorism campaign in the

---

Libya, Mali, Pakistan, the Philippines, Somalia, and Syria.University of Vienna Law Review, Vol. 2:1 (2018), pp. 69-94. https://doi.org/10.25365/vlr-2018-2-1-69. P87

Sahel region. The Obama Administration asserted in 2012 that US-conducted drone strikes were being carried out with the "full consent and cooperation" of the host states[241]. Some African presidents like President Mohamud of Somalia endorsed foreign support with drone strike in the country in order to fight al Shabaab.

However, under international law, state's consent may preclude the wrongfulness of acts that would otherwise be contrary to international law. As part of its jus ad bellum framework, Article 2(4) of the UN Charter prohibits the use of force "against the territorial integrity or political independence of any state". As such, if a foreign power deploys military force in another state's territory, but with the validly given consent of the said host state, this would not constitute a violation of the UN Charter.

International Human Rights Law and International Humanitarian Law

IHRL and IHL, consent may enable the resort to drone strikes as governed by jus ad bellum, the states concerned will still be under an obligation to ensure that these strikes do not contravene international humanitarian law and the standards of human rights law. Agnès Callamard, UN Special Rapporteur confirmed extrajudicial killings of UAV, and further posed that, the legality of a drone strike under the law regulating inter-state use of force does not say anything about its wrongfulness under IHL or human rights law[242].

Former UN Special Rapporteur on extrajudicial killings Philip Alston similarly warned that a positive obligation still rests on the consenting state to require the targeting

---

241 Ibid

242 U.N. Special Rapporteur Release Report on Drone Strikes and Soleimani Killing By Elliot Setzer. https://www.lawfareblog.com/un-special-rapporteur-release-report-drone-strikes-and-soleimani-killing

state to demonstrate that the force used will comply with applicable IHL and international human rights law. If there is any doubt as to the lawfulness of a strike that has already occurred, the host state should investigate and, in the case of a finding of wrongdoing, prosecute those responsible and seek compensation for the victims.

Foreign powers coordinating drone strikes remains under an obligation to respect applicable IHL and human rights law. The right to life, which applies both in peace time and during situations of armed conflict, extends to all "persons located outside any territory effectively controlled by the State, whose right to life is nonetheless impacted by its military or other activities in a direct and reasonably foreseeable manner"[243]. Foreign powers like the US and France are therefore under an obligation to respect this right and to conduct prompt, thorough and effective investigations into any allegations of arbitrary deprivation of life resulting from their deployment of armed drones in the territory of another state and, where appropriate, prosecute such incidents and ensure reparations for the victims.

In addition, they are required to take steps to prevent any similar violations from happening in the future. Similarly, under customary international law, states operating drone strikes in another state's territory have the duty to investigate any alleged violations of IHL resulting from these strikes, prosecute those responsible and provide reparations.

Assistance with Drone Strikes

In addition to the states directly concerned, any state providing assistance with armed drone operations may also bear responsibility under international law for any IHL or

---

243 General comment No. 36 (2018) on Article 6 of the ICCPR, on the right to life. https://www.oursplatform.org/resource/right-to-life/

human rights violations arising from lethal drone strikes. As explained above, countries including Djibouti, Cameroon, Niger, Tunisia and Italy have allowed the deployment of US drones from military bases located on their territory. This operational support is in many cases crucial to the US's drone programme in the region.

Under the International Law Commission's Draft Articles on Responsibility of States for Internationally Wrongful Acts, a state can be held responsible for assisting or being complicit in IHL or human rights violations if it does so with knowledge of the circumstances of the wrongful act, with a view to facilitating the execution of the act and if such act would be wrongful if committed by the assisting state itself. States permitting another state to carry out an armed attack against a third state from its territory may also be in breach of the prohibition of the use of force under jus ad bellum.

International human rights bodies, including the Human Rights Committee and the European Court of Human Rights, have similarly held that a state may be found responsible for extraterritorial human rights violations where it has contributed to such violations. States are thus under an obligation to assess the risks that any form of assistance with another state's drone operation could contribute to human rights or IHL violations. A similar view seems to have been adopted by the African Commission on Human and Peoples' rights when issuing its recommendations to the Nigerien government in 2018. Here, the Commission expressed its concern that US drones have "caused deaths among the civilian population" and called on Niger to ensure respect for international human rights and humanitarian law, particularly regarding the use of combat drones and carry out independent and impartial investigations into all deaths caused by drones and bring the alleged perpetrators to justice, including payment of compensation to the victims and members of their family[244].

Thus far, there have been no reports of any drone strikes in Niger. With this in mind, there is good reason to interpret the broadly formulated recommendation of the African Commission as not only placing a responsibility on Niger to make sure any drone strikes on its own territory do not violate IHL or international human rights law, but also in relation to strikes in Libya or the broader Sahel region.

In practice, however, transparency and accountability mechanisms in relation to drone strikes have been noticeably lacking. As also described above, information on civilian casualties arising from drone strikes is repeatedly withheld by governments, which often cite national security concerns. This makes it very difficult to verify whether such strikes complied with international human rights and IHL standards or whether states are fulfilling their duty to investigate.

In order to comply with their obligations under international law, foreign powers deploying armed drones as well as those states permitting such deployment on their territory should establish clear oversight mechanisms to enable independent scrutiny of any decisions authorizing armed drone use. This will allow effective parliamentary oversight and judicial review of such decisions. Greater transparency will also enable civil society organizations to carefully monitor the military use of drones and their impact on the civilian population.

---

244 Niger Facing Pressure to Ensure U.S. and French Drone Strikes Comply with Human Rights Law by Rahma Hussein, Alex Moorehead and Jonathan Horowitz. September 6, 2018. https://www.justsecurity.org/60589/niger-facing-pressure-ensure-u-s-french-drone-strikes-comply-human-rights-law/

The ongoing refusal to acknowledge civilian casualties and the further lack of transparency in relation to drone operations present a serious obstacle for any steps towards accountability and ensuring respect for the right of victims of unlawful drone strikes to a remedy. Such blatant denial of justice and redress to victims may increase feelings of resentment, distrust and frustration in affected communities, which in turn may contribute to further political, social and economic instability in the region.

Drone Strikes and State Responsibility: AU Perspective

According to Benjamin Ng'aru (2013), In light of the Glomar responses or the veil of secrecy by the CIA and the Pentagon's Joint Special Operations Command on the drones programme in African several human rights and international law within their territories or those of third parties were violated[245].

There are certain regional and international obligations that African states and the AU must adhere to while condoning the use of their territory as drone launch pads for global war on terror[246].

Article 3(b) of the *Constitutive Act of the AU* provides that the objective of the AU shall be to: "Defend the sovereignty, territorial integrity and independence of its Member States."[247]

---

245 Ng'aru (2013) Unmanned Aerial Vehicles: Call for an African Union resolution on the use of drones in Africa. https://africlaw.com/2013/08/05/unmanned-aerial-vehicles-call-for-an-african-union-resolution-on-the-use-of-drones-in-africa/

246 Ibid

247 Unmanned Aerial Vehicles: Call for an African Union resolution on the use of drones in Africa by Benjamin Ng'aru. https://africlaw.com/2013/08/05/unmanned-aerial-vehicles-call-for-an-african-union-resolution-on-the-use-of-drones-in-africa/

Some scholars argue that, the use of drones to attack certain non-state actors such as the Islamic Courts Union or Al-Qaeda in Somalia is impermissible because only armed attacks by state actors trigger the right to use force[248]. The International Court of Justice has given a narrow interpretation of this right, as only applicable against state actors[249]. Whereas certain elements of Al-Qaeda in Somalia have been sponsored by certain quarters of the Somali authorities, their activities cannot be wholly attributable to Somalia or even any other host state[250].

Human Rights Watch argues that for drone attacks to be justifiable, there must be an armed conflict: hostilities must be between the US and a group that is sufficiently organized and must reach a level of intensity that is distinct from sporadic acts of violence. Outside of an armed conflict, where international human rights law applies, the US can only target an individual if he poses an imminent threat to life and only employ lethal force as a measure of last resort[251].

Article 3(h) of the Constitutive Act of the AU obligates member states to:

---

248 https://www.960cyber.afrc.af.mil/News/Article-Display/Article/2353270/miniature-menace-the-threat-of-weaponized-drone-use-by-violent-non-state-actors/

249 Legal Consequences of the Construction of a Wall in the Occupied Palestinian Territory. https://www.icj-cij.org/case/131

250 Marchal, R. (2011) The Rise Of A Jihadi Movement In A Country At War. Harakat Al-Shabaab Al Mujaheddin In Somalia. https://www.sciencespo.fr/ceri/sites/sciencespo.fr.ceri/files/art_RM2.pdf

251 ARTICLE 19's submission. Response to the consultation of the UN Special Rapporteur on Freedom of Expression on her report on challenges to freedom of opinion and expression in times of conflicts and disturbances19 July 2022. https://www.ohchr.org/sites/default/files/documents/issues/expression/cfis/conflict/2022-10-07/submission-disinformation-and-freedom-of-expression-during-armed-conflict-UNGA77-cso-article19.pdf

"Promote and protect human and peoples' rights in accordance with the African Charter on Human and Peoples' Rights and other relevant human rights instruments."

Article 23(1) of the African Charter on Human & People's Rights (Banjul Charter) provides that:

"All peoples shall have the right to national and international peace and security. The principles of solidarity and friendly relations implicitly affirmed by the Charter of the United Nations and reaffirmed by that of the Organization of African Unity shall govern relations between States."

The AU and its member states have an obligation to co-operate with other states in the promotion of international peace and security as per Article 3(e) of the Constitutive Act: encourage international cooperation, taking due account of the UN Charter and the *Universal Declaration of Human Rights* (UDHR). However, the use of African states' territories such as Arba Minch in Ethiopia to launch drone strikes in Somalia or even in northern Kenya may be a violation of the objectives of the Constitutive Act by such drone-host states. The Republic of Djibouti, the Federal Democratic Republic of Ethiopia together with the Republic of Seychelles are signatories of the Constitutive Act.

Article 3 of the UDHR, provides that:

"Everyone has the right to life, liberty and security of person."

Article 6 of the *International Covenant on Civil and Political Rights* (ICCPR), provides that[252]: "Every human being has the inherent right to life. This right shall be protected by law. No one shall be arbitrarily deprived of his life."

---

252 Abolition of the Death Penalty: A Legal Anachronism! By Osamudiamen Obasogie. https://legamart.com/articles/abolition-of-the-death-penalt/

It is therefore argued that the right to life extends not only to persons who are civilians, in non-combat situations, but also to persons involved in an armed conflict.

Article 2(1) of the ICCPR to which the African states are parties provides that:

"Each State Party to the present Covenant undertakes to respect and to ensure to all individuals within its territory and subject to its jurisdiction the rights recognized in the present Covenant, without distinction of any kind, such as race, color, sex, language, religion, political or other opinion, national or social origin, property, birth or other status."

More disturbing are media reports that, persons not actively involved in hostilities such as rescuers, mourners and attendees of funerals of drone strikes victims, are deliberately targeted by subsequent drone strikes. Whereas it may be impossible to independently verify these claims, it brings to the fore, the likely extra-judicial nature of these strikes are a clear violation of Article 3 of the UDHR and Article 6 of the ICCPR at the very least.

While acknowledging the unlikely move to terminate the drone program, it is imperative that there should be accountability and respect for international human rights law as well as international humanitarian law. The time has come for African judicial bodies or even the **African Court of Human and People's Rights** to exercise their mandates to uphold and protect the rule of law and safeguard human rights in the region. The lack of a clear AU policy, or resolution at the very least, calling for a legal framework on the use of or hosting of drones in Africa is alarming.

Further, it is imperative that appropriate legal and operational structures are urgently put in place to regulate the use of drones in a manner that complies with the requirements of international law, international human rights law, international humanitarian law and international refugee law.

Conclusion

During a consultative meeting on international narrative of drone strikes, Ms. Massimino revealed that she is in favor of targeted killing as strange as that might sound from a human rights lawyer because the alternative is not an absence of killing but rather indiscriminate killing[253]. She further added that, drone precision is a is a good thing from a human rights perspective[254].

Ms. Massimino equally argued that, she is not in favor of federal court oversight of drone strikes and targeted killing, but for a special court to sanction targeted killings in advance, but those raise separation-of-powers issues and questions as to whether those courts would be improperly rendering advisory opinions[255].

However, states frequently gloss over the risks of drone warfare: the fact that the use of drones makes it easier to resort to violence and, even though drones are framed as precise, the fact that their use risks civilian casualties and conflict escalation if not embedded in a clear legal framework, with oversight and as part of a clear military strategy that goes beyond merely targeted killings. There is strong evidence that

---

253 Drone Strikes and Targeted Killings: Domestic and International Perspectives. https://www.ca2.uscourts.gov/docs/jc_reports/2014/4_Drone_Strikes.pdf

254 Ibid

255 Drone Strikes and Targeted Killings: Domestic and International Perspectives. https://www.ca2.uscourts.gov/docs/jc_reports/2014/4_Drone_Strikes.pdf

drones have killed and injured civilians in Africa. Journalists, experts and civil society groups have written about civilian casualties in Burkina Faso, Mali, Libya and Somalia.

Most Africa states do not publish ground operations; neither do they make available data for researchers in the domain of security studies. More so, there is little public disclosure about the existence of any investigations following such casualties, including any reparations provided to victims of unlawful drone strikes. This lack of transparency makes it very hard to verify whether drone attacks were carried out in accordance with IHL and IHRL. These indications of civilian casualties also underline the need for states deploying drones to put in place stronger military operational standards.

Civil society organizations and activists in the region have strongly criticized military drone alliances. States are still reluctant to provide adequate response to their citizens, but instead repress oppositional views of state military machine[256]. This ongoing secrecy by states about drone deployments in Africa and censorship of the press limits the space for civil society to engage meaningfully in a debate about drone warfare in Africa[257].

This further hinders transparency about the use of lethal force with armed drones, in particular in areas inaccessible to journalists and researchers wanting to investigate the impact of military operations. However, if African and non-African states sincerely want to stabilize regions in Africa, they need to be transparent about their military operations and be open to criticism by civil society groups, researchers

---

256 https://paxforpeace.nl/media/download/PAX_remote_horizons_FIN_lowres.pdf

257 Lethal drones are a new menace to Africa James Jeffrey. https://newafricanmagazine.com/28128/

and experts. Otherwise, the growing use of remote warfare with drones could seriously undermine legitimate security concerns and public support, and risk normalizing the use of lethal force with drones.

References

D. Gettinger, 2019, 'The drone databook. The Center for the Study of the Drone at Bard College', p. XI. Accessed at: https://dronecenter. bard. edu/files/2019/10/CSD-Drone-Databook-Web.pdf New America, 'Non-State Actors with Drone Capabilities', n.d. Accessed at: https://www. newamerica.org/international-security/reports/ worlddrones/non-state actors-with-drone-capabilities J. P. Craiger, & D. M. Zorri, JSOU Press, 2019, 'Current Trends in Small Unmanned Aircraft Systems: Implications for U.S. Special Operations Forces', p.2. Accessed at: ld.php (libguides. com)

A. Callamard, United Nations, 2020, 'Use of armed drones for targeted killings: report of the Special Rapporteur on Extrajudicial, Summary or Arbitrary Executions', p. 6. Accessed at: https://digitallibrary.un.org/record/3884890?ln=en

C. Cole, Drone Wars, 'What's wrong with drones?', 20 March 2014. Accessed at: https://dronewars.net/2014/03/20/whats-wrong-with-drones/

G. Woodhams& J. Borrie, 2018, 'Armed UAVs in conflict escalation and inter-State crisis', pp. 9-12. Accessed at: https://www.unidir.org/files/publications/pdfs/armed-uav-in-conflict-escalation-and-inter-state-crisis-en-747.pdf M. Espinoza, 2018, 'State Terrorism: Orientalism and the drone programme', 'Critical Studies on Terrorism', 11(2), 376-393, p. 380.

D. Axer, Wired, 'Hidden History: America's Secret Drone War in Africa', 2012. Accessed at: https://www.wired.com/2012/08/somalia-drones/

The Bureau of Investigative Journalism, 'Somalia: Reported US covert actions 2001-2016', n.d. Accessed at: https://www.thebureauinvestigates.com/drone-war/data/somalia-reported-us-covert-actions-2001-2017 Sims & P. Bergen, New America, 2018, 'Airstrikes and Civilian Casualties in Libya', pp.16, 17, 23. Accessed at: https://d1y8sb8igg2f8e.

Z. Rosenberg, FlightGlobal, 'France deploys Harfang over Libya', 25 August 2011. Accessed at: https://www.flightglobal.com/france-deploys-harfang-over libya/101788.article

L. Peruzzi, FlightGlobal, 'Italy flies first Predator B sortie over Libya', 15 August 2011. Accessed at: https://www.flightglobal.com/italy-flies-firstpredator-b-sortie-over-libya/101538.article. 'U.S. military personnel arrive in Niger: Obama in letter to Congress', Reuters, 22 February 2013. Accessed at: https://www.reuters.com/ article/us-usa-niger-forces/u-s-military-personnel-arrive-in-niger-obama-in-letter-to-congress-idUSBRE91L0NN20130222

Airwars, 'Somalia: Reported US covert actions: 2001-2016', n.d. Accessed at: https://airwars.org/archives/bij-drone-war/drone-war/data/somalia-reported-us-covert-actions-2001-2017.

J. Scahill, 'The CIA's Secret Sites in Somalia', The Nation, 10 December 2014. Accessed at: https://www.thenation.com/article/archive/cias-secret-sites-somalia/

J. Scahill, 'The Assassination Complex', The Intercept, 15 October 2015. Accessed at: https://theintercept.com/drone-papers/the-assassination-complex/

S. Shane & J. Becker, 'Secret 'Kill List' Proves a Test of Obama's Principles and Will', The New York Times, 29 May 2012. Accessed at: https://www.nytimes.com/2012/05/29/world/obamas-leadership-in-war-on-al-qaeda.html

The Guardian, Somali militants attack US drone base and European Convoy. Accessed at https://www.theguardian.

com/world/2019/sep/30/somali-militants-attack-us-drone-base-and-european-convoy

B. Obama, White House, 2012, 'U.S. Strategy Toward Sub-Saharan Africa', p. 3. Accessed at: https://2009-2017.state.gov/documents/organization/209377.pdf

D. Benjamin, 'LRA, Boko Haram, Al-Shabaab, Aqim, and Other Sources of Instability in Africa', U.S. Department of State, 25 April 2012. Accessed at: https://2009-2017.state.gov/j/ct/rls/rm/2012/188816.htm

The Intercept, 'Small Footprint Operations 5/13', 15 October 2015. Accessed at: https://theintercept.com/document/2015/10/14/small-footprint-operations-5-13/#page-3

N. Turse, 'The stealth expansion of a secret U.S. drone base in Africa', The Intercept, 21 October 2015. Accessed at: https://theintercept. com/2015/10/21/stealth-expansion-of-secret-us-drone-base-in-africa/

N. Turse, 'Target Africa', The Intercept, 15 October 2015. Accessed at: https://theintercept.com/drone-papers/target-africa/

M. McCord, 25 June 2015, 'Military Construction, Navy Reprogramming Request', Department of Defense United States of America. Accessed at: https://comptroller.defense. gov/Portals/45/Documents/execution/reprogramming/fy2015/milcon/15-10_MC_May_2015_Request.pdf

C. Savage & E. Schmitt, 'Trump Eases Combat Rules in Somalia Intended to Protect Civilians', The New York Times, 30 March 2017. Accessed at: https://www.nytimes.com/2017/03/30/world/africa/trump-is-said-to-ease-combat-rules-in-somalia-designed-to-protect-civilians.html

Amnesty International, 2019, 'The hidden US war in Somalia', London, UK, p. 65. Accessed at: https://www.amnesty.org/download/Documents/AFR5299522019ENGLISH.PDF

A. Entous & M. Ryan, 'U.S. has secretly expanded its global network of drone bases to North Africa', The Washington Post, 26 October 2016. Accessed at: https://www.washingtonpost. com/world/national-security/us-has-secretly-expanded-its-global-network-of-drone-bases-to-northafrica/2016/10/26/ ff19633c-9b7d-11e6-9980-50913d68eacb_story.html

P. Markey & T. Amara, 'Revolution a fading memory, economic frustrations grow in Tunisia', Reuters, 30 October 2016. Accessed at: https://www.reuters.com/article/us-tunisia-politics-insight/revolution-a-fading-memory-economic-frustrations-grow-in-tunisia-idUSKBN12U0FA

S. Spittaels, N. Abou-Khalil, K. Bouhou, M. Kartas, D. McFarland & P. Servia, United Nations Security Council, 1 June 2017, 'Final report of the

Panel of Experts on Libya established pursuant to resolution 1973 (2011)', p. 40. Accessed at: https://undocs.org/S/2017/466

C. Whitlock, 'U.S. plans to add drone base in West Africa', The Washington Post, 28 January 2013. Accessed at: https://www. washingtonpost.com/world/national-security/us-plans-to-add-drone-base-in-west-africa/2013/01/28/ce312c24-6994-11e2-aba3-d72352683b69_story.html

R. Trafford & N. Turse, 'Cameroonian troops tortured and killed prisoners at base used for U.S. drone surveillance', The Intercept, 20 July 2017. Accessed at: https://theintercept. com/2017/07/20/cameroonian-troops-tortured-and-killed-prisoners-at-base-used-for-u-s-drone-surveillance/

D. Gettinger, The Center for the Study of the Drone, 'The American drone base in Cameroon', 21 February 2016. Accessed at: https://dronecenter.bard.edu/drone-base-cameroon/

D. Leveille, The World, 'Can the US' new drone base in Cameroon help fight Boko Haram?', 1 March 2016. Accessed at: https:// www.pri.org/stories/2016-03-01/can-us-new-drone-base-cameroon-help-fight-boko-haram

Amnesty International, 2017, 'Cameroon's secret torture chambers: Human rights violations and war crimes in the fight against Boko Haram', pp. 6, 18-19, 41-43. Accessed at: https://www.amnesty.org/download/Documents/ AFR1765362017ENGLISH.PDF

N. Turse & R. Trafford, 'Pentagon denies knowledge of Cameroon base abuses — despite being aware of reports of torture', The Intercept, 31 July 2017. Accessed at: https://theintercept.com/2017/07/31/pentagon-cameroon-torture-salak-state-department/

U.S. Department of State, 2016, 'Custom report excerpts: Cameroon'. Accessed at: https://www.state.gov/report/custom/6660ca97fe-2/

Turse & Trafford, 31 July 2017. Cameroon's secret torture chambers: Human rights violations and war crimes in the fight against Boko Haram (2017). Amnesty International, 1-73. https://www.amnesty.org/en/documents/afr17/6536/2017/en/

'U.S. military personnel arrive in Niger: Obama in letter to Congress', Reuters, 22 February 2013. Accessed at: https://www.reuters.com/article/us-usa-niger-forces/u-s-military-personnel-arrive-in-niger-obama-in-letter-to-congress-idUSBRE91L0NN20130222

N. Turse, 'U.S. military surveys found local distrust in Niger. Then the air force built a $100 million drone base.', The Intercept, 3 July 2018. Accessed at: https://theintercept.com/2018/07/03/us-niger-drone-base/

C. Whitlock, 'Pentagon set to open second drone base in Niger as it expands operations in Africa', The Washington Post, 1 September 2014. Accessed at: https://www.washingtonpost.com/world/national-security/pentagon-set-to-open-second-drone-base-in-niger-as-it-expands-operations-in-africa/2014/08/31/365489c4-2cb8-11e4-994d-202962a9150c_story.html

J. Penney, 'Drones in the Sahara', The Intercept, 18 February 2018. Accessed at: https://theintercept.com/2018/02/18/niger-air-base-201-africom-drones/

H. Cooper & E. Schmitt, 'Niger Approves Armed U.S. Drone Flights, Expanding Pentagon's Role in Africa', The New York Times, 30 November 2017. Accessed at: https://www.nytimes.com/2017/11/30/us/politics/pentagon-niger-

drones.html?login=smartlock&auth=login-smartlock&login
=smartlock&auth=login-smartlock&login=smartlock&auth
=login-smartlock&login=smartlock&auth=login-smartlock

D. Flynn & A. Massalatchi, 'Niger would welcome armed U.S. drones: foreign minister', Reuters, 18 September 2013. Accessed at: https://www.reuters.com/article/us-niger-drones/niger-would-welcome-armed-u-s-drones-foreign-ministeridUSBRE98H0PW20130918

Twitter User 'Obretix', 'two MQ-9 Reaper drones at Agadez https://satellites.pro/#16.952138,8.014868,17 yesterday', [Twitter]. Accessed at:https://twitter.com/obretix/status/1299426725110185986?s=20

J. Penney, E. Schmitt, R. Callimachi, & C. Koettl, 'How a C.I.A. drone base grew in the desert', The New York Times, 9 September 2018. Accessed at: https://www.nytimes.com/2018/09/09/world/africa/cia-drones-africa-military.html

African Commission on Human & Peoples' Rights, 2018, '23rd Extraordinary session'. Accessed at: http://www.nuhanovicfoundation.org/user/file/2018_african_commission_human_peoples_rights_concluding_observations_periodic_report_niger.pdf

H. Cooper, T. Gibbons-Neff, C. Savage, & E. Schmitt, 'Pentagon Eyes Africa Drawdown as First Step in Global Troop', The New York Times, 24 December 2019. Accessed at: https://www.nytimes.com/2019/12/24/world/africa/esper-troops-africa-china.html?auth=login-email&login=email

N. Turse, 'Exclusive: The US military's plans to cement its network of African bases', Mail & Guardian, 1 May 2020. Accessed at: https://mg.co.za/article/2020-05-01-exclusive-the-us-militarys-plans-to-cement-its-network-of-african-bases/

E. Schmitt & C. Savage, 'U.S. Military Seeks Authority to Expand Counterterrorism Drone War to Kenya', The New York Times, 15 September 2020. Accessed at: https://www.nytimes.com/2020/09/15/us/politics/shabab-drone-authorities-kenya.html

Ministère de la Défense, 2013, 'French white paper: Defense and national security', p. 54. Accessed at: https://www.defense.gouv.fr/content/download/215253/2394121/White%20paper%20on%20defense%20%202013.pdf

I. Kfir, 2018, 'Organized Criminal-Terrorist Groups in the Sahel: How Counterterrorism and Counterinsurgency Approaches Ignore the Roots of the Problem', 'International Studies Perspectives', 19(4), 344-359, p. 351.

World Nuclear Association, 'Nuclear power in France', July 2020. Accessed at: world-nuclear.org/Information-Library/Country-Profiles/countries-A-F/France.aspx

R. Reeve & Z. Pelter, 2014, 'From new frontier to new normal: Counter-terrorism operations in the Sahel-Sahara', "Remote Control Project, Oxford Research Group", p. 6.

Yvan Guichaoua, 2020, 'The bitter harvest of French interventionism in the Sahel', 'International Affairs', 96(4), 895–911, p. 905.

T. Balzacq, S. Léonard, & J. Ruzicka, 2016, "Securitization' revisited: Theory and cases', 'International Relations', 30(4), 494-531, p. 509

J. Karlsrud, 2019, 'From liberal peacebuilding to stabilization and counterterrorism', 'International Peacekeeping', 26(1), 1-21, p. 15.

Oxford Research Group, 'The military intervention in Mali and beyond: An interview with Bruno Charbonneau', 28 March 2019. Accessed at:https://www.oxfordresearchgroup.org.uk/Blog/the-french-intervention-in-mali-an-interview-with-bruno-charbonneau

B. Oliveira Martins & M. Strange, 2019, 'Rethinking EU external migration policy: contestation and critique', 'Global Affairs', 5(3), 195-202.

T. Megerisi & A. Lebovich, 'France's strongman strategy in the Sahel', European Council on Foreign Relations, 8 March 2019. Accessed at:https://www.ecfr.eu/article/commentary_frances_strongman_strategy_in_the_sahel

Ministère de l'Europe et des Affaires étrangères, 'Migration', February 2019. Accessed at: https://www.diplomatie.gouv.fr/en/country-files/africa/migration/

M. Duffield, 2010, 'The liberal way of development and the development—Security impasse: Exploring the global life-chance divide', 'Security dialogue", 41(1), 53-76, pp. 62-63.

M. Asencio, P. Gros & J. Patry, Foundation pour la Recherche Strategique, 2010, 'Les drones tactiques a voilure tournante dans les engagements contemporains'. Accessed at: https://www.files.ethz.ch/isn/122387/2010_08.pdf

Ministère des Armées, 'Présentation de l'opération', 25 October 2013. Accessed at : https://www.defense.gouv.fr/operations/missions-achevees/operation-serval-2013-2014/dossier/presentation-de-l-operation

'French military to extend Mali 'counterterrorism' operations into Sahel', France 24, 13 July 2014. Accessed at: https://www.france24.com/en/20140713-france-military-serval-mali-terrorist-aqim-sahel

Ministère de la Défense, 'Opération Serval : zoom sur le détachement Harfang', 8 February 2013. Accessed at: https://www.defense.gouv.fr/actualites/operations/operation-serval-zoom-sur-le-detachement-harfang

J. Le Drian, 'Pourquoi l'armée française a un besoin urgent de drones', Les Echos, 31 May 2013. Accessed at: https://www.lesechos.fr/2013/05/pourquoi-larmee-francaise-a-un-besoin-urgent-de-drones-1097785

B. Stevenson, 'France orders third Reaper system', FlightGlobal, 17 December 2015. Accessed at: https://www.flightglobal.com/civil-uavs/france-orders-third-reaper-system/119165.article

République Française, 'LOI n° 2013-1168 du 18 décembre 2013 relative à la programmation militaire pour les années 2014 à 2019 et portant diverses dispositions concernant la défense et la sécurité nationale', 9 December 2020. Accessed at: https://www.legifrance.gouv.fr/affichTexte.do?cidTexte=JORFTEXT000028338825&categorieLien=id

S. Cvijic, L. Klingenberg, D. Goxho & E. Knight, Open Society Foundations, 2019 'Armed drones in Europe', p. 51. Accessed at: https://www.opensocietyfoundations.org/publications/armed-drones-in-europe

G. Lubold & J. E. Barnes, 'Italy Quietly Agrees to Armed U.S. Drone Missions Over Libya', The Wall Street Journal, 22 February 2016. Accessed at:https://www.wsj.com/articles/italy-quietly-agrees-to-armed-u-s-drone-missions-over-libya-1456163730

Ministero Della Difesa, 'Libya', n.d. Accessed at: http://www.aeronautica.difesa.it/missione/attivitaoperative/operazioni_concluse/opr_internazionali_concluse/Pagine/Libia.aspx

T. Kington, 'Italy Gives Bombing Stats for Libya Campaign', Overblog, 14 December 2011. Accessed at: http://rpdefense.over-blog.com/article-italy-gives-bombing-stats-for-libya-campaign-92483481.html

A. Shalal, 'U.S. government approves Italy's request to arm its drones', Reuters, 4 November 2015. Accessed at: https://www.reuters.com/article/us-italy-usa-drones/u-s-government-approves-italys-request-to-arm-its-drones-idUSKCN0ST1VI20151104

Ministero Della Difesa, 'MQ-9A Predator B', n.d. Accessed at: http://www.aeronautica.difesa.it/mezzi/mlinea/Pagine/MQ9APredatorB.aspx

P. Di Salvo, Italian Coalition for Civil Liberties and Rights, 'Armed Drones: the European Countries' Interests at Stake', 30 May 2017. Accessed at:https://cild.eu/en/2017/05/30/armed-drones-the-european-countries-interests-at-stake/

Senato Della Repubblica, 2017, 'Relazione Sullo stato della disciplina militare e sullo stato dell'organizzazione delle forze armate', p. 166. Accessed at: http://www.senato.it/service/PDF/PDFServer/DF/343378.pdf

M. Day, 'Italy will use drones and tripled sea patrols in bid to halt deadly migrant boat wrecks', Independent, 14 October 2013. Accessed at: https://www.independent.co.uk/news/world/

europe/italy-will-use-drones-and-tripled-sea-patrols-in-bid-to-halt-deadly-migrant-boatwrecks-8879844.html

'Libia, precipitato drone spia italiano', la Repubblica, 20 November 2019. Accessed at: https://www.repubblica.it/esteri/2019/11/20/news/libia_drone_italiano_precipita-241512228/

Maxalb, 'Droni, marò e parà italiani contro pirati e shebab somali', Africa ExPress, 5 March 2020. Accessed at: https://www.africa-express.info/2014/09/03/droni-maro-e-para-italiani-contro-pirati-e-shabab-somali

J. Karlsrud & F. Rosén, 2013, 'In the Eye of the Beholder? UN and the Use of Drones to Protect Civilians', 'Stability: International Journal ofSecurity and Development', 2(2), pp. 1-2. Accessed at: http://doi.org/10.5334/sta.bo

United Nations Security Council, 'Côte d'Ivoire Has Entered 'New Phase' in Consolidating Peace, But Still Faces Formidable Threats that Require Continued UN Presence, Security Council Told', 16 April 2013. Accessed at: https://www.un.org/press/en/2013/sc10973.doc.htm ;

M. Nichols, 'U.N. seeks surveillance drones for Mali, shelves plans for Ivory Coast', Reuters, 12 May 2014. Accessed at: https://www.reuters.com/article/us-un-drones-ivorycoast-mali-idUSBREA4B0R720140512

D. Gilman, OCHA Policy Development and Studies Branch, 2014, 'Unmanned Aerial Vehicles in Humanitarian Response', p. 13. Accessed at: https://www.unocha.org/sites/unocha/files/Unmanned%20Aerial%20Vehicles%20in%20Humanitarian%20Response%20OCHA%20July%202014.pdf

H. Ladsous & A. Haq, Expert Panel on Technology and Innovation in UN Peacekeeping, 2014, "Performance Peacekeeping", p. 5. Accessed at: http://www.performancepeacekeeping.org/offline/download.pdf

T. Justin, 'South Sudan: UN Doesn't Need Drones, Attack Helicopters', Voa, 18 June 2015. Accessed at: https://www.

voanews.com/africa/south-sudan-un-doesnt-need-drones-attack-helicopters

'Des drones tactiques français en Centrafrique', Le Figaro, 24 May 2017. Accessed at: https://www.lefigaro.fr/flash-actu/2017/05/24/97001-20170524FILWWW00389-des-drones-tactiques-francais-en-centrafrique.php

United Nations, n.d., 'Module 1 – MINUSCA Instructor Notes and Guidance', p. 16-17. Accessed at: http://repository.un.org/bitstream/handle/11176/400575/MINUSCA%20Instructor%20Notes%20and%20Guidances.pdf?sequence=17&isAllowed=y

A. Ahronheim, 'Did Morocco finally get their Israeli drones?', The Jerusalem Post, 3 February 2020. Accessed at: https://www.jpost.com/israel-news/did-morocco-finally-get-their-israeli-drones-616230

S. Kasraoui, 'Morocco Buys Israeli Drones to Combat Extremism in Western Sahara', Morocco World News, 3 February 2020. Accessed at:https://www.moroccoworldnews.com/2020/02/292656/morocco-buys-israeli-drones-to-combat-extremism-in-western-sahara/

'Morocco-Israel $48m arms deal', Middle East Monitor, 31 January 2020. Accessed at: https://www.middleeastmonitor.com/20200131-moroccoisrael-48m-arms-deal/

"SIPRI Arms Transfers Database," Stockholm Peace Research Institute, n.d. Accessed at: https://www. sipri.org/databases/armstransfers.

'Algeria evaluating Chinese CH-4 UAV', DefenceWeb, 11 March 2014. Accessed at: https://www.defenceweb.co.za/aerospace/aerospace-aerospace/algeria-evaluating-chinese-ch-4-uav/

'Algeria, Egypt unveil Chinese UAVs', DefenceWeb, 2 November 2018. Accessed at: https://www.defenceweb.co.za/aerospace/unmanned-aerial-vehicles/algeria-egypt-unveil-chinese-uavs/"SIPRI Arms Transfers Database," Stockholm Peace Research Institute, n.d. Accessed at: https://www. sipri.org/databases/armstransfers.

'Algeria operating new UAV types', DefenceWeb, 7 January 2019. Accessed at: https://www.defenceweb.co.za/aerospace/unmanned-aerial-vehicles/algeria-operating-new-uav-types/

'Algerian military announces armed UAV strike', Janes, 2019. Accessed at: https://www.janes.com/article/88189/algerian-military-announces-armed-uav-strike

'Tunisian Revolution', Aljazeera, 17 December 2015. Accessed at: https://www.aljazeera.com/indepth/inpictures/2015/12/tunisian-revolution-151215102459580.html

M. Peck, 'Insitu awarded Tunisian ScanEagle drone contract', C4ISRNET, 14 October 2016. Accessed at: https://www.c4isrnet.com/unmanned/uas/2016/10/14/insitu-awarded-tunisian-scaneagle-drone-contract/

UAS Vision, 'Tunisia to Receive Further ScanEagles', 21 July 2016. Accessed at: https://www.uasvision.com/2016/07/21/tunisia-to-receive-further-scaneagles/

Agence Tunis Afrique Presse, 'Le ministère de la Défense nie l'existence de bases militaires américaines en Tunisie', 27 October 2016.Accessed at:https://www.tap.info.tn/fr/Portail-%C3%A0-la-Une-FR-top/8362882-le-minist%C3%A8re-de-la-d%C3%A9fense-nie

M. Hosenball & A. Shalal, 'U.S. using Tunisia to conduct drone operations in Libya: U.S. sources', Reuters, 26 October 2016. Accessed at:https://www.reuters.com/article/us-usa-drones-tunisia-idUSKCN12Q2PW

'Polémique autour des drones américains en Tunisie', RFI, 28 October 2016. Accessed at: http://www.rfi.fr/fr/afrique/20161028-tunisie-polemique-drones-americains-libye

H. Nsaibia, 'America Is Quietly Expanding Its War in Tunisia', National Interest, 18 September 2018. Accessed at: https://nationalinterest.org/blog/middle-east-watch/america-quietly-expanding-its-war-tunisia-31492

B. E. Bekdil, 'Turkey's TAI sells six Anka-S drones to Tunisia', DefenseNews, 16 March 2020. Accessed at: https://www.defensenews.com/unmanned/2020/03/16/turkeys-tai-sells-six-anka-s-drones-to-tunisia/

L. Sariibrahimoglu, 'Roketsan chief says Tunisia interested in guided bombs for UAVs', Janes, 20 October 2020. Accessed at: https://www.janes.com/defence-news/rokestan-chief-says-tunisia-interested-in-guided-bombs-for-uavs/

Stockholm Peace Research Institute, "SIPRI Arms Transfers Database," n.d. Accessed at: https://www.sipri.org/databases/armstransfers

United Nations Security Council, 2011, 'Resolution 1970 (2011)', p.1. Accessed at: https://undocs.org/en/S/RES/1970%20(2011)

United Nations Security Council, 2011, 'Resolution 1973 (2011)'. Accessed at: https://www.un.org/securitycouncil/s/res/1973-%282011%29 North Atlantic Treaty Organization, 'NATO and Libya', 9 November 2015. Accessed at: https://www.nato.int/cps/en/natohq/topics_71652.htm

L. Trevelyan, 'Libya: Coalition divided on arming rebels', 29 March 2011. Accessed at: https://www.bbc.com/news/world-africa-12900706

L. Friese, N. R. Jenzen-Jones & M. Smallwood, Armament Research Services and PAX, 2016, 'Emerging Unmanned Threats: The use ofcommercially-available UAVs by armednon-state actors', p. 48. Accessed at: https://www.academia.edu/37605935/Emerging_Unmanned_Threats_The_use_of_commercially-available_

M. Ryan & S. Raghavan, 'U.S. remains on the sidelines in Libya's conflict as Russia extends its reach', The Washington Post, 20 July 2020.Accessed at: https://www.washingtonpost.com/national-security/us-remains-on-the-sidelines-in-libyas-conflict-as-russia-extends-itsreach/2020/07/17/04be5100-bf90-11ea-864a-0dd31b9d6917_story.html

S. Raghavan, 'In Libya, cheap, powerful drones kill civilians and increasingly fuel the war', The Washington Post, 22 December 2019.Accessed at: https://www.washingtonpost.com/world/middle_east/libyas-conflict-increasingly-fought-by-cheap-powerful-drones/2019/12/21/a344b02c-14ea-11ea-bf81-ebe89f477d1e_story.html

L. Majumdar Roy Choudhury, L. A. de Alburquerque Bacardit, A. Kadlec, M. Kartas, Y. Marjane & A. Wilkinson, United Nations Security

Council, 2019, 'Letter dated 29 November 2019 from the Panel of Experts on Libya established pursuant to resolution 1973 (2011) addressedto the President of the Security Council', p. 2. Accessed at: https://www.securitycouncilreport.org/atf/cf/%7B65BFCF9B-6D27-4E9C-8CD3-CF6E4FF96FF9%7D/S_2019_914.pdf

D. Malyasov, 'Austrian-made UAV Schiebel Camcopter S-100 Shot Down in Libya', Defence Blog, 15 January 2015. Accessed at: https://defence-blog.com/news/austrian-made-uav-schiebel-camcopter-s-100-shot-down-in-libya.html

S. Ugwuanyi, 'Controversy as Buhari commissions Air Force drone 'earlier launched' by Jonathan', Daily Post, 16 February 2018. Accessed at:https://dailypost.ng/2018/02/16/controversy-buhari-commissions-air-force-drone-earlier-launched-jonathan/

A. Fittarelli, 'Tracking the Nigerian Armed Forces' COIN offensive in North-East Nigeria', Bellingcat, 20 February 2017. Accessed at: https://www.bellingcat.com/news/africa/2017/02/20/tracking-nigerian-armed-forces-coin-offensive-north-east-nigeria/

J. Lin & P.W. Singer, 'It Looks Like An Armed Chinese-Made Drone Crashed In Nigeria', Insider, 29 January 2015. Accessed at: https://www.businessinsider.com/it-looks-like-an-armed-chinese-made-drone-crashed-in-nigeria-2015-1?international=true&r=US&IR=T

A. Famuyiwa, 'NAF Drone Destroys Boko Haram Base', 2 February 2-16. Accessed at: https://prnigeria.com/2016/02/02/naf-drone-destroysboko-haram-base/

J. Frew, Drone Wars UK, 2018, 'Drone Wars The Next Generation', pp. 21 – 22. Accessed at: https://dronewarsuk.files.wordpress.com/2018/05/dw-nextgeneration-web.pdf

J. Erunke, 'NAF aircraft destroys Boko Haram vehicle workshop,kills many', Vanguard, 17 January 2018. Accessed at: https://www.vanguardngr.com/2018/01/naf-aircraft-destroys-boko-haram-vehicle-workshopkills-many/

J. Erunke, 'NAF remote-controlled aircraft hits Boko Haram settlement, kills many', Vanguard, 29 January 2018. Accessed at: https://www.vanguardngr.com/2018/01/naf-remote-controlled-aircraft-hits-boko-haram-settlement-kills-many/

Nigerian Air Force, 'Nigerian air force remotely piloted aircraft destroys Boko Haram terrorists gun truck', 1 February 2018, [Video]. Accessed at: https://www.youtube.com/watch?v=O84MBjPqCxs

Nigeria Air Force, 'Nigerian air force remotely piloted aircraft destroys another Boko Haram terrorists artillery gun', 7 February 2018, [Video]. Accessed at: Ahttps://www.youtube.com/watch?v=PsmqGwEFnWE

A. Tauna, 'President Buhari tasks NAF on mass production, export of drones', Daily Post, 15 February 2018. https://dailypost.ng/2018/02/15/president-buhari-tasks-naf-mass-production-export-drones/

Nigerian Air Force, 'Tsaigumi unmanned aerial vehicle on exercise hard strike', 16 February 2018, [Video]. Accessed at: https://www.youtube. com/watch?v=yqKCewf1m8s

'Buhari unveils locally made drone', News Express, 15 February 2018. Accessed at: https://www.newsexpressngr.com/news/50010-Buhariunveils-locally-made-drone

G. Martin, 'Additional UAVs being acquired for the Nigerian Air Force', Defence Web, 13 October 2020. Accessed at: https://www.defenceweb.co.za/aerospace/unmanned-aerial-vehicles/additional-uavs-being-acquired-for-the-nigerian-air-force/

G. Jennings & J. Binnie, 'Nigeria receives Wing Loong II UAVs from China', Janes, 10 November 2020. Accessed at: https://www.janes.com/defence-news/news-detail/nigeria-receives-wing-loong-ii-uavs-from-china

'La guerre contre Boko Haram: le Cameroun est seul !', Camerounlink, 30 December 2014. Accessed at: http://www.camerounlink.com/actu/0/81458/0/SessionID-R9FD5UVF9ODZA5SXKKO8HEUUWT5MHK--cl1-0--cl2-0--bnid-2--nid-81458

AFCEA, 'Insitu to Provide Scan Eagle to Kenya and Cameroon', 30 September 2015. Accessed at: https://www.afcea.org/content/Blog-insitu-provide-scan-eagle-kenya-and-cameroon

S. Leberger, 'Le Cameroun utilise des drones d'observation dans la lutte contre Boko Haram', Overblog, 18 February 2015. Accessed at:http://wakatafrique.over-blog.com/2015/02/le-cameroun-utilise-des-drones-d-observation-dans-la-lutte-contre-boko-haram.html

D. N. Kouekem, 'Lutte concertée contre Boko Haram: Paul Biya et les Cameroonians disent << welcome ! >> ', Journal du Cameroun.com, 20October 2015. Accessed at: https://www.journalducameroun.com/lutte-concertee-contre-boko-haram-paul-biya-et-les-cameroonians-disentwelcome/

M. Bakoa, 'Paul Biya reçoit l'ambassadeur des Etats-Unis au Cameroun', Cameroon Tribune, 6 November 2015. Accessed at: http://ct2015.cameroon-tribune.cm/index.php?option=com_content&view=article&id=93322:paul-biya-recoit-llambassadeur-des-etats-unis-au-cameroun-michael-stephen-hoza&catid=1:politique&Itemid=3

'US flies drones from Ethiopia to fight Somali militants', BBC News, 28 October 2011. Accessed at: https://www.bbc.com/news/world-africa-15488804

'US shuts drone base in Ethiopia', BBC News, 4 January 2016. Accessed at: https://www.bbc.com/news/world-africa-35220279

A. Egozi, 'Ethiopian Army to get BlueBird UAVs', Flight International, 11 April 2011. Accessed at: https://www.flightglobal.com/news/articles/ethiopian-army-to-get-bluebird-uavs-355404/

S.Y. Mengesha, 2016, 'Ethiopia: Silencing Dissent', 'Journal of Democracy', 27(1), 89-94, p. 93. Accessed at: https://muse.jhu.edu/article/607619/pdf

W. Zwijnenburg, 'Are Emirati Armed Drones Supporting Ethiopia from an Eritrean Air Base?', Bellingcat, 19 November 2020. Accessed at https://www.bellingcat.com/news/rest-of-world/2020/11/19/are-emirati-armed-drones-supporting-ethiopia-from-an-eritrean-air-base/

S. Weinberger, 'China has already won the drone wars. May 10, 2018 Foreign Policy. Accessed at https://foreignpolicy.com/2018/05/10/china-trump-middle-east-drone-wars/

Peter Dorrie, 2014, 'Sudan's Drones Are Dropping Like Flies'. War is Boring. Accessed via https://medium.com/war-is-boring/sudans-drones-are-dropping-like-flies-ffa1be165291; Jonathan Hudson, 2012, 'Sudan Armed Forces Implicated in Video Captured by Their Own Drones.

Satellite Sentinel Project. Accessed via http://satsentinel.org/blog/sudan-armed-forces-implicated-video-captured-their-own-drone

United Nations Security Council, 15 January 2019, 'Letter dated 15 January 2019 from the Chair of the Security Council Committee pursuant to resolutions 1267 (1999), 1989 (2011) and 2253 (2015) concerning Islamic State in Iraq and the Levant (Da'esh), Al-Qaida and associated individuals, groups, undertakings and entities addressed to the President of the Security Council', p. 23. Accessed at: https://www.un.org/sc/ctc/wp-content/uploads/2019/02/N1846950_EN.pdf

International Centre for Counter-Terrorism – The Hague, 'Recording ICCT Live Briefing: Al-Qaeda and the Islamic State: Competition or Cooperation in Western Sahel?', 26 March 2020, [Video], 49:00 – 51:00 min.

International Centre for Counter-Terrorism – The Hague, 26 March 2020, [Video], 52:20 – 53:30.

S. Crino & A. Dreby, Small Wars Journal, 'Drone Technology Proliferation in Small Wars', 10 February 2019. Accessed at: https://smallwarsjournal.com/jrnl/art/drone-technology-proliferation-small-wars

D. Searcey, 'Boko Haram is back. With better drones.', The New York Times, 13 September 2019. Accessed at: https://www.nytimes.com/2019/09/13/world/africa/nigeria-boko-haram.html

United States Department of State Publication, 2019, 'Country Reports on Terrorism 2018', p. 293. Accessed at: https://www.justice.gov/eoir/page/file/1215411/download

'Mali: à Indelimane, l'armée était en alerte', RFI, 5 November 2019. Accessed at: http://www.rfi.fr/fr/afrique/20191105-mali-indelimane-armee-etait-alerte

Josh Rogi, ''Somali president asks for more American help'', Foreign Policy, 18 January 2013, available under https://foreignpolicy.com/2013/01/18/somali-president-asks-for-more-american-help/ .

Max Byrne, 'Consent and the use of force: an examination of 'intervention by invitation' as a basis for US drone strikes in Pakistan, Somalia and Yemen', 'Journal on the Use of Force and International Law', Vol. 3, No. 1, 2016, p. 117

Violent non-state actors are also referred to as non-state armed actors/groups (NSAA/G) or terrorist organizations; these are groups partially or completely independent from state governments and use or threaten violence to achieve their goals. Examples: Terrorist groups such as Hamas, Hizballah, al-Qaeda, ISIL(S), Boko Haram, and others.

Amy E. Smithson, "Rethinking the Lessons of Tokyo," in *Ataxia: The Chemical and Biological Terrorism Threat and the US Response* (Washington, DC: Henry L. Stimson Center, 2000), 80.

"Non-State Actors with Drone Capabilities," *New America*, www. newamerica.org/international-security/reports/world-drones/non-state-actors-with-drone-capabilities/.

Adiv Sterman, "Hezbollah Drones Wreak Havoc on Syrian Rebel Bases." *The Times of Israel*, 21 Sept. 2014, www.timesofisrael. com/hezbollah-drones-wreak-havoc-on-syrian-rebel-bases.

David Hambling, "ISIS is Reportedly Packing Drones with Explosives Now," *Popular Mechanics*, December 16, 2015, http://www.popularmechanics.com/military/weapons/ a18577/isis-packing-drones-with-explosives/.

Joby Warrick, "Use of Weaponized Drones by ISIS Spurs Terrorism Fears," *Washington Post*, 21 February 2017, https://www.washingtonpost.com/world/national-security/use-of-weaponized-drones-by-isis-spurs-terrorism-fears/2017/02/21/9d83d51e-f382-11e6-8wd72-263470bf0401_story.html?utm_term=.11aab1591ca9.

Adiv Sterman, "Hezbollah Drones Wreak Havoc on Syrian Rebel Bases," *The Times of Israel*, 21 September 2014, www. timesofisrael.com/hezbollah-drones-wreak-havoc-on-syrian-rebel-bases/.

"Exclusive: IS Group's Armoured Drones Attack from the Skies in Battle for Raqqa," France 24, 26 June 2017, www.france24. com/en/20170626-syria-exclusive-raqqa-drones-islamic-state-group-battle.

David Axe, "Great, Mexican Drug Cartels Now Have Weaponized Drones," *Vice*, 25 October 2017, https://www.vice.com/en_ us/article/j5jmb4/mexican-drug-cartels-have-weaponized-drones.

DJI – Based out of Shenzhen, China, DJI it is the world's leading producer of consumer drone technology.

"DJI Matrice 600 Pro," DJI Store, https://store.dji.com/product/ matrice-600-pro.

Christoph Koettl and Barbara Marcolini, "A Closer Look at the Drone Attack on Maduro in Venezuela," *New York Times*,

10 August 2018, www.nytimes.com/2018/08/10/world/americas/venezuela-video-analysis.html.

Tim Shipman, "Al-Qaeda Terror Group Returns to Target Airliners and Airports," *Sunday Times*, 23 December 2018, www.thetimes.co.uk/article/al-qaeda-terror-group-returns-to-target-airliners-mlj3lgf87.

Amar Toor, "Paris Has a Drone Problem," *The Verge*, 26 February 2015, www.theverge.com/2015/2/26/8113291/paris-drone-uav-eiffel-tower-charlie-hebdo.

Michael Schmidt and Michael D. Shear, "A Drone, Too Small for Radar to Detect, Rattles the White House," *New York Times*, 26 January 2015, www.nytimes.com/2015/01/27/us/white-house-drone.html.

Don Rassler, *Remotely Piloted Innovation: Terrorism, Drones, and Supportive Technology* (West Point, New York: Combating Terrorism Center, 2016), https://ctc.usma.edu/wp-content/uploads/2016/10/Drones-Report.pdf.

Don Rassler, Muhammad Al-`Ubaydi, and Vera Mironova, "The Islamic State's Drone Documents: Management, Acquisitions, and DIY Tradecraft," Combating Terrorism Center at West Point, 31 January 2017, ctc.usma.edu/ctc-perspectives-the-islamic-states-drone-documents-management-acquisitions-and-diy-tradecraft/.

Matthew Gault, "How the Islamic State Gets Its Drones," *Vice*, 13 July 2018, www.vice.com/en_us/article/gy3bzx/how-the-islamic-state-gets-its-drones.

Don Rassler, *The Islamic State and Drones: Supply, Scale, and Future Threats* (West Point, New York: Combating Terrorism Center, 2018), https://ctc.usma.edu/wp-content/uploads/2018/07/Islamic-State-and-Drones-Release-Version.pdf.

Karl Mueller et al., "The Nature of Escalation," in Forrest E. Morgan et al., *Dangerous Thresholds: Managing Escalation in the 21st Century* by (Santa Monica, CA: RAND Corporation, 2008), 7–45, https://www.rand.org/pubs/monographs/MG614.html.

Robert J. Bunker, *Terrorist and Insurgent Unmanned Aerial Vehicles: Use, Potentials, and Military Implications* (Carlisle, PA: Strategic Studies Institute, US Army War College Press, 2015), https://scholarship.claremont.edu/cgi/viewcontent.cgi?article=1050&context=cgu_facbooks.

Fariha Karim, "Terror Trial Told of Isis Drone Plot," *The Times*, 11 September 2019, 20, https://www.thetimes.co.uk/article/hisham-muhammad-terror-trial-told-of-isis-drone-plot-fp2tm0689.

Joseph A. Beninati, "Examining the Cyber Operations of ISIS," Order No. 10108064, Utica College, 2016, Ann Arbor: ProQuest, Web, 18 December 2019, https://hssonline.org/wp-content/uploads/2017/08/ISISdiss77-10-4444-COMPLETE-2-08.29.2017.pdf.

Jordan N. Galehan, "Gender and the Enactment of Suicide Bombings by Boko Haram." Order No. 13901011, Southern Illinois University at Carbondale, 2019, Ann Arbor: ProQuest, Web, 18 December 2019, https://opensiuc.lib.siu.edu/cgi/viewcontent.cgi?article=2713&context=dissertations.

Stephanie Werner, "How the Use of Violent and Non-Violent Strategies Influence the Effectiveness of Terrorist Organizations," Order No. 13884680, Webster University, 2019, Ann Arbor: ProQuest, Web, 18 December 2019.

Ross Furneaux et al., "Drone Terrorism Is Now a Reality, and We Need a Plan to Counter the Threat," World Economic Forum, www.weforum.org/agenda/2018/08/drone-terrorism-is-now-a-reality-and-we-need-a-plan-to-counter-the-threat.

Vesna Markovic, "Suicide Squad: Boko Haram's Use of the Female Suicide Bomber," *Women & Criminal Justice* 29, no. 4-5 (2019): 283–302,https://doi.org/10.1080/08974454.2019.1629153.

ABOUT THE AUTHOR

Mr. Saron Messembe Obia is a security expert and international consultant. He is a counter terrorism analyst of Islamic Theology of Counter Terrorism-ITCT, a UK based Counter Islamist Terrorism Think Tank. A Member and Ambassador for African Continent of Global Socio-Economic and Financial Evolution Network-GSFEN. He has also worked with the International Association for Counter Terrorism and Security Professional South East Asia-IACSP SEA, as Assistant Editor and IACSP SEA Representative for Cameroon Publication Division. He studied Criminology and Security Management (PGD), Security Studies (MSc) at the Pan African Institute for Development West Africa- PAID-WA and a certified Public Policy Analyst at the Nkafu Policy Institute. He has authored several articles on cyber security, counter terrorism, stadia security, money laundering, human rights and jihadists tendencies in Sub Saharan Africa and Europe, as well as books; 'The Criminal Mind in The Age of Globalization', 'What Is Putin Doing? Russia-Ukraine Crisis. Sanctions, Peace and Security in the 21st Century' and 'Jihadist Tendencies in West Africa: Boko Haram's Game – Yesterday, Today and Tomorrow'.